SpringerBriefs in Economics

SpringerBriefs present concise summaries of cutting-edge research and practical applications across a wide spectrum of fields. Featuring compact volumes of 50 to 125 pages, the series covers a range of content from professional to academic. Typical topics might include:

- A timely report of state-of-the art analytical techniques
- A bridge between new research results, as published in journal articles, and a contextual literature review
- A snapshot of a hot or emerging topic
- An in-depth case study or clinical example
- A presentation of core concepts that students must understand in order to make independent contributions

SpringerBriefs in Economics showcase emerging theory, empirical research, and practical application in microeconomics, macroeconomics, economic policy, public finance, econometrics, regional science, and related fields, from a global author community.

Briefs are characterized by fast, global electronic dissemination, standard publishing contracts, standardized manuscript preparation and formatting guidelines, and expedited production schedules.

More information about this series at http://www.springer.com/series/8876

Bruno S. Frey

Economics of Art and Culture

Springer

Bruno S. Frey
CREW - Center for Research in Economics
and Well-Being
University of Basel
Basel, BS, Switzerland

ISSN 2191-5504 ISSN 2191-5512 (electronic)
SpringerBriefs in Economics
ISBN 978-3-030-15747-0 ISBN 978-3-030-15748-7 (eBook)
https://doi.org/10.1007/978-3-030-15748-7

Library of Congress Control Number: 2019935489

This Springer imprint is published by the registered company Springer Nature Switzerland AG
The registered company address is: Gewerbestrasse 11, 6330 Cham, Switzerland

Preface

This booklet provides an introduction to the relationships between the arts and the economy and to the application of economic thinking to the arts.

The content is influenced by former contributions of the author to the economics of art, published in various scholarly journals, collections of articles, and books of his own. He admits to a fondness for unconventional ideas and proposals, such as replicating the most important churches, palaces, monuments, and canals of Venice at a new location with all possible digital extensions in an effort to save the original Venice from further destruction.

The author is European; this is reflected in the text. Though quite widely travelled, with extensive stays in North and South America, Australia, and China, he is most familiar with classical Western art. Therefore, this kind of art is most frequently considered, but he is confident that much of it is also directly relevant to other cultures.

The author is grateful to Dr. Simon Milligan and to Evelyn Holderegger for carefully checking the manuscript and for many good suggestions for improvement. He also benefitted from having the opportunity to discuss some aspects of the economics of art with Dr. Andreas Spillmann, Director of the Swiss National Museum, and with Dr. David Iselin, art economist.

Basel, Switzerland
Bruno S. Frey

Contents

Part I
Introduction

Chapter 1
What Is the Economics of Art and Culture?

Abstract The economics of art and culture is a fascinating and worthwhile subject. Its analysis is based on the economic way of thinking. It deals with a large number of diverse issues, such as how valuable art is to society, how the art market and auctions work, the specific characteristics of artists' labour market, and the role of copies and fakes in art. Various areas of the arts and culture are analyzed, such as opera and theatre, festivals, films, museums, cultural heritage and cultural tourism. Finally, various aspects of the public support for the arts are studied, and it is shown that art makes people happy.

Keywords Economics of Art · Economics of Culture · Cultural Economics · Economic approach · Non-user benefits · Non-economic values · Human motivation · Mass culture · Commercialization · Democracy · Market

1.1 A Challenging Discipline

The economics of art, also called the economics of culture, is a relatively little-known area of the science of economics. Often it is not even known to professional economists, let alone to practitioners active in culture.

The economics of art can be understood in two different ways:

(1) *The relationship of arts with the economy*, that is, the interaction between two important parts of society.
This relationship is rather evident. Everyone knows that a great deal of money is needed to run an opera house; that many artists are poor—while some have become very rich; and that paintings and other works of art are auctioned, sometimes reaching huge prices. Important areas analysed in art economics are the performing arts (theatres, operas and films, festivals), the visual arts (in particular art auctions), and the many different kinds of museums, cultural industries, cultural tourism, and cultural heritage.
(2) *The application of economic thinking to the area of the arts and culture.*
This approach to the social sciences represents a totally new kind of *interdisciplinarity*. Until now, this term has been understood to indicate a combination

B. S. Frey, *Economics of Art and Culture*, SpringerBriefs in Economics,
https://doi.org/10.1007/978-3-030-15748-7_1

of various disciplinary approaches. In contrast, the economic approach uses the particular way economists look at social issues. They carefully distinguish between what people want (their preferences) and their opportunities for reaching these goals (the constraints imposed by material means and by legal and political institutions). People are assumed to act primarily in a way that satisfies their goals. The rational choice approach provides a systematic study of the interaction between the behaviour of individuals and institutions existing in society. It has been successfully applied to many areas such as politics and political economy, the family, education, the natural environment, terrorism, sports, and happiness.

One of the most fascinating applications of the economic approach has been to the arts. It actually has quite an old history but it was not known by this name in the past). Economists in German-speaking countries were long interested in economic aspects of the arts. Public finance issues received special attention, in particular the role of the state in financing culture.

On the whole, it was taken for granted that the public should subsidize the arts, as they produce what would today be called positive external effects on the society at large. These externalities are called "non-user benefits" because they also accrue to people not consuming a particular cultural activity, but to the population at large. Famous British economists such as Lord John Maynard Keynes, Lord Lionel Robbins or Sir Alan Peacock were actively engaged in the arts both theoretically and practically.

The birth of art economics as a discipline of its own within modern economic science can be dated to the publication of Baumol and Bowen's book *Performing Arts—The Economic Dilemma* in 1966. The dilemma referred to is created by an ever-increasing level of per capita income and the concomitant increase in the cost of staging the performing arts: theatres and operas. As a result, the performing arts are under continually rising financial pressure. It seems that, precisely because societies are rich and become ever richer, they have ever more problems in entertaining the living arts.

Subsequent to the publication of Baumol and Bowen's influential book, cultural economics began to flourish. In recent decades, the literature on the economics of art has expanded greatly. There are now many excellent survey articles, textbooks, and collections of articles.

The study of the economics of art has been institutionalized by the Association for Cultural Economics International, which regularly organizes conferences and edits a review entitled the *Journal of Cultural Economics*. The bulk of articles relating to the subject are published there, but some contributions also appear in other journals.

The economic approach to the arts has close relationships with that of other disciplines. In particular, the sociology of art is in many respects quite similar. In contrast, contacts with art history have so far been limited. This may be due to a misunderstanding of the economic approach. Art historians seem to think that economists only value what is profitable in monetary terms, and that they therefore propose to commercialize art. Art historians are surprised to hear that most economists favour state support of the arts and go to great pains to empirically demonstrate "non-economic" values such as existence, prestige, education, and bequest values. There are first signs of promising efforts to bridge the gap between art history and art economics, particularly with respect to cultural property.

1.2 The Scientific Approach

The dominant rational choice methodology has proved most useful in the study of culture: it is based on a clear behavioural model, and this helps to capture the demand and supply of art. On the basis of the resulting equilibria, it is possible to derive empirically testable implications. Most of the predictions conform to "common sense", but others are unexpected and surprising. An example is the analysis of the performing arts: the richer societies become, the more difficult it is for them to maintain live performing arts.

It is useful to take into account that individuals do not always and under all conditions act in a rational way. In particular, psychological aspects are important to consider. Behavioural anomalies are sometimes important in cultural realm. For example, many owners of paintings become subject to the *endowment effect*: they are not prepared to sell a painting for a given sum, say 10,000 Euros, though they would not buy it for that price, even disregarding transaction costs. This behavioural anomaly is likely to influence prices paid in auctions and elsewhere.

Another important contribution of psychology to art economics refers to human motivation. There is no doubt that artists systematically respond to monetary (i.e. extrinsic) incentives, like all other people. Salvador Dalí is reported to have said, "All that interests me is money"; statements to the same effect have been made by several other artists. Nevertheless, strong evidence exists that successful artists have had a strongly developed intrinsic motivation: they pursue art for art's sake. This applies particularly to the first years in an artist's career. Commonly, this is the most innovative and productive period in an artist's life. The extent to which, and the specific ways in which an artist is motivated intrinsically or extrinsically, are crucial when it comes to the public support of culture. These considerations are relevant to the question whether public subsidies, in particular direct income transfers to individual artists, raise or damage creativity. To focus on both extrinsic and intrinsic motivation and to look at the dynamic interaction between the two (termed the *crowding effect*) is crucial both for understanding and supporting the arts.

1.3 Fascinating Issues

Many applications of economic thinking to culture yield fascinating insights. Sometimes, however, such applications might simply rename observations in economic terminology. Transgressing established boundaries and venturing into new methodological territory allows us to gain novel and challenging insights. Indeed, art economics is one of those areas in economics most open to new approaches. Perhaps more than in other areas, such an exchange of views is fruitful in the arts.

In order to illustrate that art economics is indeed fascinating, two issues are briefly discussed, namely whether the market is bound to produce bad art, which many people believe, and whether cultural decisions can be left to democratic decisions, an idea which many art lovers abhor.

1.3.1 Does the Market Produce Bad Art?

Most people believe that the market produces low-quality art. Complaints about "mass culture" and "commercialization" abound. This view dominates not only amongst the general public, but perhaps even more strongly in intellectual discussions. Behind this deep-seated conviction is a general suspicion of the market on the part of intellectuals, and also the more specific belief that public support of culture is needed to maintain high quality. Not only must the state subsidize the arts, but it must also produce cultural activities by running museums, theatres, opera houses, ballet companies, and orchestras.

The popular view that the market only produces low-quality mass culture is based on a misunderstanding of how the market works. Moreover, it is empirically incorrect. In fact, the market *can* produce high quality culture, and even art of the highest quality. To understand this statement, it is necessary to look behind the market. The market is an institution that responds to demand. If low-quality art is asked for, it produces low-quality art—but if high-quality art is demanded, it produces high-quality art. There is no reason to assume that such a demand for high-quality culture does not exist. In reality, we observe that many people indeed spend money to enjoy good art. A case in point is the many art festivals, including film festivals, where art of the highest quality is presented. Such festivals are normally the result of private initiative, with the intention of avoiding the political, administrative, and artistic constraints typical of government-run theatres, opera, and concert halls. Some of these festivals cater for a small minority of lovers of a particular art form, such as modern music, which does not find a sufficiently large audience in the established artistic venues. The market thus does *not* require a mass audience. The general and wildly popular statement that "the market produces bad art" is thus untenable.

The positive consequences of competition among the demanders of art is, for instance, clearly visible for music in the age of the baroque, in which no copyrights existed for musical works. Italy and Germany, where many princes competed for composers, produced a large number of major artists such as Vivaldi, Schütz, Teleman, Händel, and Johann Sebastian Bach. In contrast, more unified France and Great Britain produced far fewer composers of high distinction.

It cannot be denied that much commercially produced art is of low, if not very low, quality. But this is not surprising. Many people may have such tastes, and the market simply reflects these. This tendency may be reinforced in some cases by economies of scale. They allow the production of large quantities at a lower price than small quantities. Nevertheless, we observe that the same market also produces serious music of superb quality, for instance in recordings of classical music. It is therefore important not to focus only on the mass aspects of the market but to see that the price system is normally well able to cater for high-quality demand.

One of the market's great advantages is that it permits and fosters *variety*. No commission and no group of experts need to approve the tastes reflected in the market. This raises the chances that innovative ideas spring forth, keeping art lively. An open market is an antidote to a monopoly of artistic taste.

The markets for art as they exist in reality are far from ideal: they suffer external effects, increasing returns, and monopolistic tendencies among suppliers. The market should be seen in perspective. For the arts, as elsewhere, several decision-making mechanisms are available. Instead of jumping to the conclusion that the government is the only entity that should support the arts, one must engage in comparing the advantages and disadvantages of the various decision-making mechanisms.

Let us now turn to another fascinating system, democracy, and its role for the arts.

1.3.2 Can Arts Policy Be Left to Democracy?

There is a common charge against "democratizing" the arts, in particular against leaving decisions about art to the people via popular referenda. The idea is that "people do not understand what good art is". It is even claimed that the people's taste in art is terrible. Therefore, cultural decisions should not be left to the members of the public.

These arguments are similar to those raised against using the market in culture. But the charge is more serious, if democratic decisions are identified with majority decisions. Such decisions are feared to inevitably lead to bad art. It is concluded that the élite must decide. This immediately raises the question: which élite? There are many possibilities:

Elected politicians. The taste of politicians does not correspond to that of the population at large (they are, on average, better educated), but it is doubtful whether they really have better judgment concerning art. Moreover, in order to secure re-election, politicians respond to a large number of outside influences. In a democracy with stiff competition between the parties, the politicians seek to fulfil the preferences of the electorate. In such a case, decisions on art are shifted back from the élite, here the politicians, to the population at large. In most democracies, however, politicians have room for discretion when making decisions on art. But it is exactly this capacity that makes it worthwhile for interest groups to influence them. The better these groups are organized, the stronger is their influence. This applies equally to art decisions, where established and therefore essentially culturally conservative group interests have a larger say than those promoting innovative forms of culture. The latter are, almost by definition, less organized and therefore politically weak, as they represent future, still unknown forms and types of art.

Art administrators in government. People employed in government and various public art organizations are generally well educated in art, but they also have a particular stake in that art. Art administrators have an interest in defending established art. Most importantly, they have an incentive to fight off outsiders—but this is exactly where creative and innovative art comes from. Leaving cultural decisions to art administrators introduces a marked conservative bias.

The private art establishment. Art critics in the media, art historians, gallery owners, and private and corporate collectors, comprise this type of élite. Many of them have a conservative slant because the art presently in vogue is their area of competence. They would partly or totally lose this advantage if an innovative art form were to appear. Consequently, real outsiders, whose raison d'être is to reject existing art, are not supported. If this happens, innovative elements tend to be lost.

This situation has partly changed since the time when the art establishment in Paris rejected the new art forms of Impressionism and Expressionism. Today, groups of people and firms actively seek to identify the newest waves in art and fashion to exploit this insider knowledge. This benefits new art forms that appear to be exploitable over a reasonably short period, but works against new art forms where this is not the case.

Artists. Decisions about culture could be left to the artists producing it. This sounds quite convincing, but only at first sight. First of all, it is far from clear whether artists are good judges of art produced by other artists. They highly value what they do themselves (otherwise they presumably would not do it), but they are sometimes quite negative about what others do. Such a reaction may be due partly to envy but even more importantly to an incapacity to go beyond their own realm of thinking: many artists are quite self-centred, a fact intimately related to their own creative efforts. However, in modern times most artists are part of rather closed social groups, which often meet with each other and assemble and exhibit in the same places.

There is yet another problem with leaving decisions on art to artists, which also applies to decisions by the art establishment: How are the decisions to be made? If representatives are to be elected, they are likely to lose touch with the groups whose tastes they are supposed to reflect. As a result, the representatives may deviate ever more from what they are supposed to reflect. This is a classical principal-agent problem.

The role of democracy for the arts may also be seen in a quite different perspective. So far, decisions on art have been discussed as being taken in the current politico-economic process. The perspective shifts fundamentally if one moves to the level of the constitution or, more generally, the level of the basic rules of society, which determine how the current decisions on art are to be taken. One of the most important constitutional rules for a flourishing cultural life is to guarantee artistic freedom. Anybody who feels that he or she wants to engage in a cultural activity should be free to do so, provided it does not impose major costs on other people. It would be too simple to assume that artistic creativity can only exist under democratic conditions so defined: some great art has been produced under authoritarian rulers. An example is the Renaissance, which was accompanied by an explosion of artistic talent. The then-reigning princes were far from democratic, but it may still be argued that the artists gained a considerable measure of artistic freedom in that period. Many of the great masters, among them Michelangelo Buonarroti and Leonardo da Vinci, were free enough to bargain with various masters. They were thus able to work for the master who provided them the most artistic freedom relative to financial compensation. Nevertheless, in our modern world, where the population as a whole and in particular artists have experienced a rise in self-determination brought about by democracy, a decision-making system involving the whole population is the best-equipped to establish and to safeguard constitutional rights for artistic freedom.

1.4 Conclusion

Looking at the arts and culture from an economic point of view provides many new and interesting insights. In many ways, this view differs fundamentally from more conventional treatments of the subject, in particular as undertaken by art historians. It is certainly not claimed that the economic approach is the only reasonable one but it offers a noteworthy alternative perspective. Many generally accepted views are challenged, such as that the market is incompatible with the arts and leads to bad outcomes, or that cultural decisions should not be left to democratic decisions but must be undertaken by a well-educated élite.

Related Literature

The extension of economics beyond the economy has been championed by

Becker GS (1976) The economic approach to human behavior. Chicago University Press, Chicago

See also, more recently,

Frey BS (1999) Economics as a science of human behaviour. Towards a new social science paradigm. 2nd rev. and extended ed., Kluwer Academic Publishers, Boston, Dordrecht and London.

The founders of the modern Economics of Art are

Baumol WJ, Bowen WG (1966) Performing arts, the economic dilemma; a study of problems common to theater, opera, music and dance. The Twentieth Century Fund Study, Hartford CT

Peacock AT (1993) Paying the Piper. Culture, Music and Money. Edinburgh University Press, Edinburgh

Survey articles are

Blaug M (2001) Where are we now in the cultural economics? J Econ Surveys 15(2):123–143
Throsby D (1994) The production and consumption of the arts: a view of cultural economics. J Econ Lit 32(1):1–29

Much of the content in the present booklet is more extensively treated in the excellent textbooks by

Throsby D (2010) The economics of cultural policy. Cambridge University Press, Cambridge
Towse R (2010) A textbook of cultural economics. Cambridge University Press, Cambridge

Other textbooks are, for instance

Benhamou F (1996) L'économie de la culture. Editions La Découverte, Paris
Frey BS, Pommerehne WW (1989) Muses and markets: explorations in the economics of the arts. Blackwell Publishers, Oxford
Gottschalk I (2006) Kulturökonomik: Probleme, Fragestellungen und Antworten. Verlag für Sozialwissenschaften, Wiesbaden
Hutter M, Throsby D (2011) Beyond price. Value in culture, economics, and the arts. Cambridge University Press, Cambridge
Towse R (2014) Advanced introduction to cultural economics. Edward Elgar, Cheltenham UK and Northampton, MA, USA

There are several comprehensive collections of articles, also dealing with aspects not covered in the present booklet:

Ginsburgh, VA, Throsby D (eds) (2006, 2014) Handbook of the economics of art and culture. Volumes I and II. Elsevier, Amsterdam.
Towse R (ed) (2003) A handbook of cultural economics. Edward Elgar, Cheltenham UK and Northampton, MA, USA

Other collections of articles are

Ginsburgh VA, Menger P-M (eds) (1996) Economics of the arts. Selected essays. Elsevier/ North Holland, Amsterdam
Klamer A (ed) (1996) The value of culture. On the relationship between economics and arts. Amsterdam University Press, Amsterdam
Peacock AT, Rizzo I (eds) (1994) Cultural economics and cultural politics. Kluwer Academic Publishers, Dordrecht
Towse R (ed) (2007) Recent developments in cultural economics. Edward Elgar, Cheltenham UK and Northampton, MA, USA
Towse R (ed.) (1997) Cultural economics: the arts, the heritage and the media industries. Edward Elgar, Cheltenham U.K. and Lyme, USA

Some monographs are, for example

Frey B (2003) Arts and economics. Analysis and cultural policy. 2nd edn. Springer-Verlag, Berlin, Heidelberg, New York
Mossetto G (1993) Aesthetics and economics. Kluwer Academic Publishers, Dordrecht and Boston
Throsby D (2001) Economics and culture. Cambridge University Press, Cambridge

Closely related sociological contributions are

Bourdieu P, Dardel A (1966) L'Amour de l'Art: Les Musées et leur Public. Editions de minuit, Paris
DiMaggio PJ (ed) (1986) Nonprofit enterprise in the arts. Oxford University Press, New York and Oxford
Foster, AW, Judith RB (eds) (1989) Art and society. Readings in the sociology of the arts. State University of New York Press, Albany.

The role of competition in classical music is analysed in

Baumol WJ, Baumol H (1994) On the economics of musical composition in Mozart's Vienna. J Cult Econ 18(3):171–198
Vaubel R (2005) The role of competition in the rise of Baroque and Renaissance music. J Cult Econ 29(4):277–297

Part II
Aspects

Chapter 2
The Social Value of Art

Abstract Most people engaged in culture favour impact studies, which measure the economic benefits produced by artistic projects. On that basis, many art expenditures seem to be economically beneficial. In contrast, art economists focus on measuring the social values produced. They include the external effects of artistic activities not taken into account by the market: existence, option, bequest, prestige, and education values. The two approaches consider different aspects of cultural management, and both must be taken into account.

Keywords Impact studies · Multiplier effect · Art expenditures · External effects · Non-use values · Non-market effects · Willingness-to-pay · Existence value · Option value · Bequest value · Prestige value · Education value

2.1 Contrasting Views

2.1.1 Impact Studies

"Arts people", those involved in the arts as politicians, public officials, private suppliers, or artists, are fond of impact studies. They favour analyses that measure the economic benefits produced by artistic projects. These analyses consider the direct expenditures going to suppliers and the indirect expenditures by visitors to an art project. The expenditures by the first recipients induce a *multiplier effect*, raising the total economic impact two to three times. Expenditures for culture therefore are likely to appear to be economically beneficial.

Consider the case of a classical opera festival to be established. The direct expenditures benefit the artistic and administrative personnel engaged in the project and the suppliers of goods and services. The recipients of direct expenditures create indirect benefits in turn by spending a large part of their revenues to supply these goods and services. Thus, the provider of costumes for the singers must spend money to produce them. The recipients of those expenditures again spend a large part of it. The visitors to the opera festival also spend money in addition to the entrance fee, for instance on transport costs, hotels, meals, hairdressers, and clothes. Thus, a multiplier process is

B. S. Frey, *Economics of Art and Culture*, SpringerBriefs in Economics,
https://doi.org/10.1007/978-3-030-15748-7_2

set in motion by the establishment of the opera festival, and this process goes well beyond the direct expenditures.

2.1.2 Capturing Non-market Benefits of Art

In contrast, arts economists focus on willingness-to-pay studies that measure the external effects, which are those effects of artistic activities not taken into account by the market. A carefully selected representative sample of individuals is asked how much they would be prepared to pay to preserve the cultural good in question.

Arts economists favour willingness-to-pay studies because they seek to measure whether the total social benefits created by the artistic project outweigh the total social costs. If it turns out that the net benefits are negative, the art project should not be undertaken, as society is worse off with it than without it. The market captures some of the benefits and costs, most importantly by visitors' paying an entrance fee to attend an artistic activity, in our example the festival. As the visits are voluntary, it makes sense to assume that people only pay the entrance fee to attend the festival, if the benefits outweigh the costs. But the market does not capture part of the benefits and costs. In particular, some positive external effects accrue above and beyond direct benefits. These effects increase people's welfare in ways that are not captured in monetary terms.

This often means that the arts project is not commercially viable, but society's welfare would be increased by its existence.

Examples of such benefits beyond market values include

- *existence value*: people benefit from the arts, even if they never attend a theatre performance or never visit a museum. They enjoy the fact that art is created and performed, even if they themselves do not engage in it as producers or consumers;
- *option value*: people do not participate in the arts at the present time but want the guarantee that they have the opportunity to do so in the future;
- *bequest value*: while not attending artistic activities themselves, parents want their children to have the opportunity to enjoy the arts in the future if they wish;
- *prestige value*: the arts, for instance a famous opera house or museum, may contribute to the recognition of a city or region and therefore provides social value;
- *education value*: the arts may be seen as contributing in a positive way to the education of young people.

All these values are disregarded by the market because people do not pay to reap those benefits. They nevertheless produce social value, which is revealed by representative surveys.

The willingness-to-pay approach is based on classical welfare analysis. The underlying idea is that, with a perfect market, a (potentially) welfare-maximizing use is made of the economic resources available to society. When the market is not perfect, there is a case for public intervention. The government should rectify the shortcomings of the market. In the example of an opera festival, the suppliers of the festival should receive a subsidy from the government amounting to the size of the positive external benefits created. This intervention is designed to overcome the otherwise inexistent, or negligible, funding for the arts project.

2.1.3 Different Views

That two such contrasting attitudes co-exist is rather surprising. Arts people focus more on the economic effects of the arts than economists do. Conversely, arts economists concentrate more on the artistic aspects than arts people do. They consider impact studies to be inappropriate and methodologically weak and even argue that impact studies may render a disservice to the arts.

The two views are rather isolated from each other. Arts people often pay considerable sums of money to commission impact studies. They rarely commission studies designed to evaluate the value of culture not reflected in market prices. They disregard such willingness-to-pay or contingent valuation studies and, at best, consider them to be purely academic exercises. On the other hand, art economists have undertaken hundreds of studies in which they make an effort to measure the value of art to society.

The two conflicting approaches focus on quite different aspects, and each relies on a different analysis and methodology:

- Arts people are convinced, and consider it as a matter of course, that art is most valuable for society. They take it as obvious that art and culture contribute to human welfare. Consequently, the support of the arts is considered as one of the essential tasks of governments. The real problem is to activate decision-makers to actually undertake artistic projects. Arts people feel that the decision-makers can best be convinced to support the arts when it is demonstrated to them that this yields large economic benefits. Impact studies serve to prove this claim "scientifically".
- Arts economists find it essential to establish the need for government support of any art project. According to classical welfare economics, a necessary condition is that the project in question produces external effects not captured by the market. Only then there is a consistent argument for government support. If there are no external effects, the artistic project can be produced by the market, provided the social benefits are larger than the social costs. Willingness-to-pay studies are the best method to identify these external effects. Art economists find it sufficient to offer their empirically based insights about whether there are external effects to legitimize government intervention.

At the level of political decision-making, both views play an important role. It is indeed crucial for willingness-to-pay studies to establish the need for government intervention. If not, the market can perform the activities more cheaply and efficiently. But it is also crucial that the projects are actually undertaken. This requires political activation. However, both approaches need to be undertaken with care. Unfounded demands for government support threaten to backfire, because many non-artistic projects also easily qualify for government support, overburdening public funds. The same occurs if it can easily be shown that the market can readily supply the artistic project in question. Political activation induced by impact studies is equally crucial, as it overcomes one of the major weaknesses of willingness-to-pay studies, the separation between evaluation and decision.

Arts people assume that the people who directly and indirectly benefit from the festival support its establishment politically. This support is based on the economic advantages gained, and is quite independent of the artistic benefits created by the artistic project.

2.1.4 Evaluation

Both arts people and arts economists consider only limited goals and seek to attain their respective goals in inadequate ways. The strengths and shortcomings of both impact studies and willingness-to-pay studies should be considered carefully.

Arts people that believe in impact studies and wish to activate decision-makers to support arts projects take into account only a part of the underlying motivation. By focusing on the expenditure effects, arts people implicitly assume that decision-makers respond solely to the economic benefits of such projects. However, people's motivational structure is much broader.

People are prepared to support artistic activities for diverse reasons, selfish economic benefits being only one, and perhaps not even the most important one. An important reason for supporting the arts is an intrinsic interest in art. People enjoy arts activities for themselves as well as for their heirs and other people. These are exactly the benefits captured by the willingness-to-pay techniques. They should therefore be of interest to arts people, especially as people with such an intrinsic love of the arts are often prepared to make a great effort to influence the political process in favour of the arts.

People that benefit commercially in a direct way from an artistic project do not necessarily support it. They may expect other projects to give them even higher profits. From a commercial point of view, a sporting event, such as a football championship, may be preferable to a classical music festival. To rely solely on the economic benefits of an artistic endeavour, as done when calculating impact values, is therefore dangerous. To rely on the commercial benefits when arguing for an arts project means that the argument is lost if a non-arts project is shown to yield even higher benefits. In that case, an impact study is counterproductive.

To rely solely on the values generated by willingness-to-pay studies is also inadequate, again because some motivational aspects are disregarded. The basic idea that arts projects' positive external effects constitute a case for government intervention does not take into account the specific incentives of governmental decision-makers. These decision-makers pursue their own goals, which are not identical or even compatible with general social welfare. Politicians pursue their own utility. A love of the arts is only one, and probably not very important, consideration; others are income, prestige, and power. Most importantly, government politicians in a democracy must be re-elected, and in an authoritarian or dictatorial system must cling to power. This means that, in election times, the politicians in power have only limited, if any, interest, at least in "high" art, which is known to be appreciated only by a small proportion of the electorate.

Public officials may exhibit a more continuous interest in the arts because they do not depend on re-election. Nonetheless, they derive utility from being able to become active in the way they best see fit, which is not necessarily best for the arts. Bureaucratic interventions in the form of public subsidies have strings attached, which are inimical to artistic freedom. Consequently, the basic idea of classical welfare economics that government interventions serve to overcome the misallocation due to external effects is politically naive. Indeed, it may even happen that government intervention worsens the state of the arts. It is therefore not sufficient to demonstrate that an arts project produces positive external effects. Rather, it is necessary to analyse how these values enter the political process and to what extent they are taken into account.

The discussion reveals that the approaches of both arts people and arts economists are valuable and needed, but that both are lacking in important respects. Both need to be extended to better reach their respective goals: activating the political process in impact studies and overcoming market failure in the willingness-to-pay studies.

2.2 Conclusion

Most people engaged in culture favour impact studies, which measure the economic benefits produced by artistic projects. These studies consider the expenditures going to suppliers and the expenditures by visitors to an art project. The additional expenditures induced by the first recipients raise the total economic impact measured. On that basis, many art expenditures seem to be economically beneficial.

In contrast, arts economists focus on willingness-to-pay studies, which measure the external effects of artistic activities not taken into account by the market. These include existence, option, bequest, prestige, and education values. The market disregards these aspects because people do not pay to reap those benefits. They nevertheless produce social value, which is revealed by the representative surveys.

The two approaches consider different aspects of cultural management, and both must be taken into account.

Related Literature

This chapter is partly based on

Frey BS (2005) What values should count in the arts? The tension between economic effects and cultural value. Working paper series/Institute for Empirical Research in Economics No. 253, University of Zurich

Valuable discussions of impact and willingness-to-pay studies are

De la Torre M (ed) (2002) Assessing the values of cultural heritage: research report. Getty Conservation Institute, Los Angeles

Journal of Cultural Economics (2003) "Contingent Valuation in Cultural Economics". Special Issue: 27(3/4):155–315. In particular the articles by

Noonan DS (2003) Contingent valuation of cultural resources: a meta-analytic review of the literature. J Cult Econ 27(3/4):159–176
Throsby D (2003) Determining the value of cultural goods: how much (or how little) does contingent valuation tell us? J Cult Econ 27(3/4):275–285

Practical applications of willingness to pay and contingent valuation include, for example

Hansen TB (1997) The willingness-to-pay for the royal theatre in copenhagen as a public good. J Cult Econ 21(1):1–28
Santagata W, Signorello G (2000) Contingent valuation of a cultural public good and policy design: the case of 'Napoli Musei Aperti'. J Cult Econ 24(3):181–204

Chapter 3
Art Markets and Auctions

Abstract Art uses labour and capital. These resources are scarce. As a result, opportunity costs arise. Cultural consumers have to make a choice between various supplies of art. In a well-functioning market, supply and demand balance. Art markets, in particular auctions, are characterized by large risks that rarely exist in other markets. These relate to authenticity, attribution, quality, and theft. Some unexpected market changes may also occur. Behavioural anomalies such as ownership bias and home bias are prominent. Investment in art diversifies a portfolio. The most sensible strategy is to buy for love of art.

Keywords Cultural consumers · Opportunity cost · Market-makers · Auctions · Record prices · Risk · Authenticity · Attribution · Quality · Theft · Behavioural anomalies · Diversification · Taxation · Money laundering

3.1 Producers and Consumers of Art

Both works of art and art performances are produced using resources. These are most importantly the labour or human capital used and the investment in new ideas or creativity. These resources are scarce and, if not employed in the arts, they can be used elsewhere. As a result, opportunity costs arise. For instance, an artist could use his or her skills in some other function, say as a decorator.

Art production is strongly affected by the changing tastes of art consumers. To be successful, a great deal of flexibility is needed. In addition, many art producers are subject to intense financial problems. In many cases, cultural producers cannot supply their goods and services at a profit. They are in constant need of public support, a sponsor, or a donor. As a result, diverse people are engaged in the arts: cultural workers, for-profit enterprises, not-for-profit firms, and many sorts of public cultural institutions. International organizations such as the UN, UNESCO, OECD, and non-governmental organizations (NGOs) play a substantial role.

The consumers of art are also subject to limitations. They are constrained by their income and wealth, and they also have limited credit. As a result, they have to make a choice between cultural activities. Many of them have to choose whether to

B. S. Frey, *Economics of Art and Culture*, SpringerBriefs in Economics,
https://doi.org/10.1007/978-3-030-15748-7_3

attend an opera performance or to buy a painting. In addition to the demand exerted by individuals, much demand also comes from consumer organizations and in particular from government agencies.

3.2 Equilibrium Between Supply and Demand

In a perfect market, prices lead to a balance in the quantity of supply and demand. If supply exceeds demand, price decreases; if demand exceeds supply, price rises, leading to an equilibrium between supply and demand. Many art markets are imperfect, partly because would-be consumers are ill informed, or because demand cannot be fully adjusted to supply. Some art activities are subject to discontinuities. An opera house cannot perform only part of an opera, even if the theatre is not fully occupied. Lowering the entry price is not simple and may be risky, because the customers who booked first may get angry. The theatre may then lose future customers.

Art markets are also characterized by market-makers, who are often charismatic leaders able to induce consumers to buy art objects or to attend a cultural event. They try to establish a monopoly or quasi-monopoly in the sector in which they are active. Professional arts associations endeavour to restrict entry into a market and so often support these quasi-monopolies. Market-makers try to impose restrictions, for instance by requiring theatre companies to only hire actors with a closely defined formal education in that profession. Such rules serve to restrict competition by outsiders. Regulations open the possibility of engaging in price discrimination in the supply of cultural goods. Consumers closely following the proposals made by the market leaders can be charged a higher price than others less affected.

Markets in culture are subject to a great many regulations imposed by governments and quasi-official institutions, such as professional associations. Examples include

- health and safety rules at work (for instance restricting the number of hours of work, which may conflict with artistic requirements);
- censorship (in many countries it is forbidden to perform some theatrical plays for reasons of state security or public decency);
- heritage (many museums, theatres, and monuments are closely protected so that no changes to structures are allowed);
- intellectual property (a cultural supplier must observe copyrights in works of art in both the performing and the visual arts).

3.3 Auctions

In the art world, auctions have always played an important role. This is clearly visible in the great attention received by record prices for the sales of paintings.

Table 3.1 shows most expensive works of art ever sold at an auction.

Table 3.1 Record prices for paintings auctioned, 2018

1.	Leonardo da Vinci's *Salvator Mundi* or *Saviour of the World*	$ 450.3 million	2017
2.	Pablo Picasso's *The Women of Algiers* (*Version O*)	$ 179.4 million	2015
3.	Amedeo Modigliani's *Nu couché*	$ 170.4 million	2015
4.	Amedeo Modigliani's *Nu couché* (*sur le côté gauche*)	$ 157.2 million	2018
5.	Francis Bacon's triptych *Three Studies of Lucian Freud*	$ 142.4 million	2013
6.	Edvard Munch's pastel *The Scream*	$ 119.9 million	2012
7.	Pablo Picasso's *Young Girl with a Flower Basket*	$ 115.0 million	2018
8.	Jean-Michel Basquiat's 1982 *Untitled*	$ 110.5 million	2017
9.	Pablo Picasso's *Nu au Plateau de Sculpteur*	$ 106.4 million	2010
10.	Andy Warhol's *Silver Car Crash* (*Double Disaster*)	$ 105.4 million	2013

These are high prices for single paintings. In particular, Leonardo da Vinci's *Salvator Mundi* reached an auction price of $ 450 million, more than two and a half times the previous maximum for Pablo Picasso's *Women of Algiers*.

These paintings were all traded at Christie's or Sotheby's in New York. In contrast to the exact figures officially documented at auctions, the values of private sales are often not revealed. But according to media reports, a painting by Willem de Kooning and one by Paul Gauguin were each sold for $ 300 million in 2015.

Specific aspects characterize art auctions, in particular pertaining to the risk involved. Generally, risk is higher in what has been called "alternative" markets, for instance in antiques, wine, stamps, and coins, than in stocks, bonds, or real estate. Two closely related terms are "emotional investment" and "investment of passion". These refer to jewellery, antique cars, and racehorses. Such investments have some typical characteristics: The current market value is difficult to evaluate; compared to financial assets, such objects are more illiquid; their value may be less correlated with stocks and bonds; the information needed before investing is quite demanding; and the transaction costs of purchase and sale tend to be high.

The art market shares all of these characteristics. In particular, works of art are typically unique, or nearly so. In recent decades, this market has come somewhat closer to the ideal of a perfect market. An increasing share of investors, in particular art investment funds, solely seek financial profit in the art market. Moreover, the information on art transactions and prices, freely and easily available on the Internet, contributes strongly to making the market more open and flexible.

3.4 Types of Art Market Risks

The art market is characterized by specific and large risks not existing in other markets, or at least not to such a significant degree. This is reflected, for instance, in the large differences in art investment returns between countries. The following four types of risk may be distinguished.

3.4.1 Risks Inherent in Works of Art

- *Authenticity.* A work of art bought in the art market may not be the original but a copy or an outright fake. The technical means to identify the fakes have continued to improve, but forgers have been equally quick to adapt. Not even art experts can guarantee that a painting is an original. It has been claimed that the art market is full of fakes. It is rumoured that there are 3000 authentic works by Camille Corot, yet there seem to be more than 8000 Corot paintings in the United States alone.
- *Attribution.* It is not always clear whether a work is by a master himself, was produced in his studio, belongs to the circle, is in the school, or is only in the style of a grand master, but this is crucially important for the price it fetches. An example is the painting *Daniel in the Lions' Den* attributed to Peter Paul Rubens and auctioned in 1882 for £ 1680 by Christie's London, and then resold for £ 2520. The painting was then attributed to Jacob Jordaens, and was therefore auctioned in 1963 for merely £ 500. In 1965 it was acknowledged as a work painted in the school of Rubens and was acquired by the Metropolitan Museum of Art in New York for £ 178,000.
- *Quality and material destruction.* It is important to know whether a work of art has been damaged in the past and repaired. Such interventions are often difficult to identify but have a significant effect on prices. Works of art are sensitive to all kinds of influences, such as light, temperature, and humidity. A well-known example is Damian Hirst's 4.3 m long tiger shark: immersed in formaldehyde in a vitrine, this proved difficult to conserve. Fire, earthquakes, and inappropriate handling by collectors and their employees may also destroy art works. An example is the *Fettecke* by Joseph Beuys, which he installed in the Düsseldorfer Kunstakademie in 1982 and which in 1986 was thrown away by a member of the cleaning staff, who thought it was dirt. In addition, damage can result from wars and civil uprisings.
- *Theft.* With rising art prices, the theft of art has become increasingly lucrative. Well-known examples include the theft of the *Mona Lisa* from the Louvre in 1911, the *Scream* by Eduard Munch from the Munch museum in Oslo in 2004, several important impressionist and expressionist paintings by Cézanne, Monet, Degas, and van Gogh from the Museum of the Bührle Foundation in Zurich in 2008, and paintings by Picasso, Matisse, Braque, Modigliani, and Léger from the Musée d'Art Moderne de la Ville de Paris in 2010. Less is known about thefts from private collectors, but it seems likely that they also happen quite often. They

are not publicly reported due to shame and fear of negative publicity. Little-known paintings may be sold on the black market, but today it is impossible to sell a famous painting or other work of art on an official market. Therefore, the thieves threaten to destroy the painting if a ransom is not paid.

3.4.2 Unexpected Market Changes

- *Holding costs*. The cost of owning a work of art is affected by the cost of storing, protecting, and insuring it. These changes may come inadvertently. For instance, if due to a spectacular theft a strong increase in the premiums for insuring a work of art unexpectedly occurs, investment in art becomes less attractive. The costs of insuring a work of art are substantial, and the annual premium usually lies between 0.1 and 0.5% of the artwork's value.
- *Government interventions*. The politicians in power may decide to raise property or sales taxes specifically for artworks. Both interventions reduce demand for art due to the higher costs, decreasing the returns on art. Similarly, governments can change export regulations for art works. This occurs even in well-established markets and in stable and democratic political environments; governments may also change property rights in works of art. A work of art may have been bought in the past according to then-existing legal provisions. Nevertheless, the government may later declare it to have been acquired illegally. An even more severe government intervention is to confiscate objects of art without any, or inadequate, compensation. The reasons adduced may be that it clashes with religious, racial, or national feelings.
- *Transaction costs*. The government may unexpectedly restrict international sales of works of art. In particular, the export of art may be prohibited, even for objects not clearly in the national interest. The holders of such works of art suffer a considerable loss, as they are unable to sell them outside of the country. They may fetch higher prices on the international market than on the local market. The international art market is still dominated by big players controlling large proportion in an oligopolistic competition. A rise in the commissions charged by influential auction houses and art dealers can lead to an immediate reduction in the returns on art.

The death of a painter or sculptor leads to yet another type of risk. Death has two opposing effects on art prices:

- *Scarcity effect.* The artist's oeuvre is fixed in quantity (at least if fakes are left out of account). If the demand for an artist's work increases, prices will rise.
- *Reputation effect.* Due to death, an artist can no longer advertise his or her work by showing it at exhibitions, using classical and social media, or drawing attention by purposely creating scandals of some sort.

According to empirical research, the death of young artists tends to reduce the price of their work. If their death was no surprise but was expected, this fact is already capitalized in the prices paid. Artists dying young have had fewer opportunities to engage in advertising their work. In contrast, the effect of the death of older artists on prices is positive: the scarcity effect dominates.

3.4.3 Behavioural Anomalies

Individuals do not always maximize their utility, nor do firms always maximize profits. Such anomalies exist in all spheres of life and all markets. There are good reasons to assume that they are stronger in art markets than in financial markets, where the level of information of market actors is more complete. Moreover, the personal preferences and idiosyncrasies of individuals play a larger role and are competed away by market forces to a lesser degree.

Predicting tastes and fashions accurately is almost impossible. Art experts have often erred in this regard. Art is extremely heterogeneous, personal preferences play a major role, and there are strong perception effects. Moreover, art does not have an intrinsic value. The fundamental value of financial assets usually provides a lower bound in the discounted future net earnings and in immediately saleable tangible assets such as engines, tools, and simple cash. Even more importantly, tastes in the arts are not immutable but the result of various types of discourse. This may lead to a consensus based on personal interactions rather than a personal evaluation.

The *ownership bias* is certainly of major importance in art and is often expressed by collectors. Once an art object is in their possession, they value it more highly than if it does not belong to them. Museum directors and curators are also strongly affected by it. This is partly due to the psychological effect of possessing works of art but also for institutional reasons. Many museums are prohibited by law from selling any item in their collection. Others do not want to sell because the directors fear being heavily criticized if the work sold later rises in price. They may also fear that in the future they will not be bequeathed any art collections because the givers want them to be held together.

The *home bias* has been shown to be highly relevant in the arts. Many collectors of paintings, stamps, and collectibles focus on works from their own country even if similar or better pieces of the same school from other countries are available at lower prices.

Herding behaviour of buyers and sellers certainly occurs in the art market. Actors follow the lead of well-known art experts, art dealers, collectors, and art museums, because they believe that these individuals and institutions are better informed about the market and its likely future development. Herding behaviour cannot be predicted; if it were, it would be avoided or exploited, resulting in the dissolution of the effect.

3.5 Why Do People Invest in Art?

Risk is particularly high in the art market, especially compared to financial assets such as stocks and government bonds. Nevertheless, there are various reasons why investments in the art market are undertaken, beyond considering the return on investment.

3.5.1 Diversification

One of the basic tenets of investment is not to put all the money in a single basket. Research shows that during the second half of the last century the art market was not closely correlated with the financial market. Sometimes there is even a negative relationship: when financial assets lose value, investors turn to other assets such as real estate and art. The weak positive or even negative correlation allows investors to diversify and reduce the overall investment risk.

3.5.2 Biased Information

Some people rely on media reports in which record prices are extensively discussed, such as the more than $ 450 million paid for da Vinci's *Salvator Mundi* in 2017. Such news is biased, because losses incurred on the art market are rarely reported. If a work of art is offered for sale but fails to attract a buyer at the right price, the seller will not advertise this fact for fear of lowering the perceived value of the work further. Auction houses refuse to feature works of art that are not likely to sell at a higher price than originally bought. Art price indices, of which there is a considerable number, do not reflect these aspects and therefore present an overly optimistic picture of the financial revenue to be made on art markets. As a result, would-be investors in art may well be misinformed.

3.5.3 Taxation and Money Laundering

The rates of taxation may differ between types of investment. In many countries, wealth in the form of art is subject to a lower tax rate than are financial assets. This is due to tax authorities finding it easier to monitor financial and real estate transactions than art dealings. The possession of art objects is often hidden. In addition, art investments may also serve to transform dubiously acquired money into a socially recognized form, facilitating tax evasion and even money laundering.

3.5.4 Conspicuous Consumption and Art Investment

An important motivation to buy art is to impress others and to raise one's social status. This also applies to political units and countries. It has become a common policy to found a well-regarded museum.

3.5.5 Love of Art

The most secure reason to buy and hold art objects is the intrinsic pleasure to be derived from viewing and owning them. The financial risk due to fluctuations in value is irrelevant to this motive. Indeed, many collectors, at least traditional ones, never think of selling their collections or even parts of them.

However, some of the risks discussed above may strongly affect art lovers. This is particularly true of the material destruction, theft, or confiscation of art one possesses. This holds even if an insurance company or the government "compensates" the art enthusiast with money. The former owners' feeling of psychological loss tends to be far greater. It is strongly felt because the collector has developed a personal relationship with the work of art. In this sense, true art lovers run an especially high risk when they buy a work of art.

3.6 Conclusion

The art market presents many more types of risk than investments in traditional financial products such as lacking authenticity, unclear attribution, material destruction, and theft. In addition, unexpected changes, for instance unforeseen government interventions, make it impossible to predict art prices accurately. Even if overall risk is higher than in other markets, and on average the expected financial return is low, art is a good option for diversifying a portfolio and an excellent investment for art lovers.

Related Literature

This chapter is partly based on

Frey BS, Cueni R (2014) Special risks in the art market. Unpublished ms, University of Zurich

A pathbreaking contribution is

Baumol WJ (1986) Unnatural value: or art investment as floating crap game. American economic review (Papers and Proceedings of the American Economic Association), 76(2):10–14

Various contributions on art markets and auctions are included in the textbooks and handbooks listed in the first chapter.

Recent empirical analyses include

Dimson E, Spaenjers C (2014) The investment performance of art and other collectibles. In: Dempster A (ed) Risk and uncertainty in the art world. Bloomsbury, London, pp 219–238
Frey BS, Eichenberger R (1995) On the rate of return in the art market: survey and evaluation. Euro Econ Rev 39(3–4):528–537
Klamer A (2014) Without uncertainty, there is no art market. In: Dempster A (ed) Risk and uncertainty in the art world. Bloomsbury, London, pp 275–286
Renneboog L, Spaenjers C (2013) Buying beauty: on prices and returns in the art market. Manage Sci 59(1):36–53
Spaenjers C (2010) Returns and fundamentals in international art markets. Job market paper

The death effect is studied in

Ursprung HW, Wiemann C (2011) Reputation, price and death: an empirical analysis of art price formation. Econ Inq 49(3):697–715

Behavioural anomalies are discussed in

Frey BS (2001) Inspiring economics. Human motivation in political economy. Edward Elgar, Cheltenham UK and Northampton, MA. USA
Frey BS, Eichenberger R (1994) Economic incentives transform psychological anomalies. J Econ Behav Organ 23(2):215–234
Goodwin J (2008) The international art markets: the essential guide for collectors and investors. Kogan Page, London

Chapter 4
The Artists' Labour Market

Abstract Not all artists are poor, but the inequality of incomes is marked. On average, artists receive lower incomes than people in other occupations. A few superstars earn high incomes. This leads to great inequality among artists. Artists with high incomes are often among the best artists. Various determinants of artists' earnings have been identified. Talent, or creativity, is very important, but belonging to a well-established artistic network, training in a prestigious school and luck also matter greatly. Artists are considerably more satisfied with their work than non-artists, mainly because they are intrinsically motivated and enjoy autonomy.

Keywords Artists' incomes · Awards · Superstars · Winner-take-all markets · Celebrity · Rich artist · Poor artists · Starving artists · Artistic networks · Intrinsic motivation · Creativity · Happiness

4.1 Starving or Rich Artists?

The figure of the starving artist is highly popular and has become the subject of art itself. A case in point is Karl Spitzweg's *Der arme Poet*, painted in 1839, which is one of the best-known paintings, at least in German-speaking countries. It depicts an artist living under miserable conditions in an attic but who is totally devoted to writing poetry. This painting has strongly shaped the views people hold about the material conditions of artists. Another well-known artistic representation of the poor conditions of artists is Giacomo Puccini's opera *La Bohème*.

At the same time, it is quite obvious that some artists have gained celebrity status and correspondingly large incomes. Examples include

- *Painters*:
  Pablo Picasso, Marc Chagall, and presently Damian Hirst, Jeff Koons, Jasper Johns, David Choe, and Gerhard Richter;
- *Opera singers*:
  Enrico Caruso, Benjamin Gigli, Elisabeth Schwarzkopf, Maria Callas, and more recently Luciano Pavarotti, Placido Domingo, Cecilia Bartoli and Anna Netrebko;

B. S. Frey, *Economics of Art and Culture*, SpringerBriefs in Economics,
https://doi.org/10.1007/978-3-030-15748-7_4

- *Popular singers*:
  The Beatles, Madonna, Celine Dion, Beyoncé, Lady Gaga, Bruce Springsteen, Johnny Mathis, Julio Iglesias, Justin Bieber, and Cher;
- *Conductors*:
  Wilhelm Furtwängler, Karl Böhm, Herbert von Karajan, Leonard Bernstein, Sir Colin Davis, and Claudio Abbado.
- *Authors*:
  J. K. Rowling, James Patterson, Dan Brown, Stephen King, Jackie Collins, Paula Hawkins, Nora Roberts, Salmon Rushdie, and Gore Vidal.

In the past too, artists of the highest renown often received substantial incomes. Examples in literature include William Shakespeare, Johann Wolfgang von Goethe, Friedrich Schiller, Victor Hugo, Molière, Charles Dickens, and Rudyard Kipling; among musicians, Georg Friedrich Händel, Joseph Haydn, and Wolfgang Amadeus Mozart; among painters, Leonardo da Vinci, Michelangelo, Raphael, Titian, Lucas Cranach, and Rembrandt.

These observations allow us to draw two conclusions:

- Not all artists are poor, but the inequality of incomes is marked;
- Artists with high incomes have not necessarily produced bad art. Indeed, they are often among the best artists.

4.2 Why Do People Become Artists?

People engage in an artistic career because this is what they deeply want to do. This intrinsic motivation holds especially for youngsters. A clear example is all those young girls who dream of becoming a prima ballerina.

Another reason to become an artist is the social recognition gained in that profession, which is far more highly appreciated than some "bourgeois" occupation. This effect is strengthened when somebody becomes a celebrity in the art world. Some people expect to gain a high income in the arts, such as musicians who form a band, hope to become famous, and so become rich.

These motivations are strong and lead to an excess supply of artists. In many, if not most artistic areas, more people are willing to work for the mostly low income to be gained. Artists are risk-loving individuals, and in this respect similar to entrepreneurs. When supply exceeds demand, the organizations that hire artists have a wide choice. In this situation, personal contacts, a network of relationships, the "right" school and education, and the skills of the agents employed by an artist are crucial.

4.3 Who Is an Artist?

There is a wide spectrum of jobs in the cultural sector, but not all can claim to be undertaken by artists. Managers, administrators, and electricians employed in that sector rarely qualify as artists, as they could do the same work in some other sector of the economy.

Artists can be defined in several ways. This can be based on the time spent on artistic work; the amount and share of income derived; the reputation among experts and/or the public; the recognition enjoyed among other artists; the quality of art produced; membership of a professional art association; education in artistic skills; and personal self-evaluation by a would-be artist.

According to most definitions, the number of artists has grown strongly in recent decades. According to the US Census, in 1940 400,000 respondents considered themselves to be artists, or 0.7% of the labour force. By the year 2000 this figure had grown almost fivefold, to 1,900,000, and doubled to 1.4% of the work force. Some of these people are self-employed, which is typical for painters and authors, while others are employed by a cultural organization, as is typical for actors and singers.

4.4 Income

Artists may gain income in the arts market, through patronage, or from various government sources. The many studies that empirically analyse the income situation of artists come to a common conclusion: Artists receive lower mean income than people of similar age, the same gender, and the same number of years of education. This also holds for median income, which is the income of the people in the middle of the population counted from above and below. There are also indications that this inequality has increased in recent times.

Many artists do not earn sufficient income to lead a decent life. They therefore engage in better-paid jobs, often teaching. In the extreme, people who consider themselves to be artists take up full-time jobs. An often-reported example is that of taxi drivers who dream of becoming opera stars.

Various determinants of artists' earnings have been identified. Talent, or creativity, is certainly very important, but it is difficult or even impossible to observe independent of the income gained. A technique called selective matching indicates the importance of belonging to a well-established artistic network or team. Training also matters greatly; its effect on income depends on the type, content, and prestige of the schools attended. Finally, luck also plays a role; being in the right place at the right time can be decisive.

4.5 Awards

In the cultural sector, awards play an important role. This is especially the case if a prize is accompanied by a sum of money. Many independently working artists, such as writers, painters, musicians, and composers are only able to survive in their profession if they regularly receive an award of money. Prizes without money are also crucial for artists' careers. This is, for instance, clearly visible in the curriculum vitae of opera singers offered to the public, which often is largely filled by the awards received. In this case, an award serves as a certification for having performed particularly well in the past.

The best-known artistic award is certainly the Nobel Prize in Literature, bequeathed every year. But there are many other highly publicized awards, such as the Academy Awards, or Oscars, given for various contributions to films (best director, best actor and actress, best supporting roles, best screenplay writer, etc.). Film festivals such as Venice, Cannes, and Locarno also award much-coveted prizes, including for life achievements. Writers can win the UK Man Booker Prize, the French Prix Goncourt, and virtually thousands of other awards.

Awards differ from purely monetary compensation in various respects. Most importantly, awards are always given in often sumptuous public celebrations attended by the media. Much care is given to identify the specific reasons why a prize has been awarded to a particular person. This raises the artists' intrinsic motivation to pursue and to further excel in their profession.

4.6 Superstars and Winner-Take-All Markets

A few very successful artists earn high income and win most of the prestigious awards. They dominate the activities in which they engage. This leads to great inequality among artists. The superstar, in most cases, is more talented than the rest, but the crucial point is that this translates into huge differences in income and public attention. There are two reasons for this striking inequality:

- Consumers of cultural activities are unwilling to substitute greater talent for lesser talent, even if the latter is cheaper. Several books written by mediocre writers do not add up to one book by a first-rate writer. Moreover, there is a large number of artists in every field, but consumers are unable to remember a large number of them; normally they focus on the three or four most famous ones. As a result, the demand for the top artists is very high, while artists of only slightly less talent remain far less observed and compensated.
- Modern technology supports and strengthens the concentration on the few top performers. In earlier times, an opera singer may have been a great star in the opera house of her town. It did not much matter that in a nearby city there was a singer with greater talent. With the advent of digitization, this situation has changed

completely. Now everybody can enjoy the performance of the world-best singer through films, records, radio, television, and the many outlets in the new media.

The phenomenon of superstars relates to winner-take-all markets. They are characterized by a few artists dominating supply—though they rarely take everything. Artists are active in an intensely competitive market, and only a tiny fraction of them will succeed in terms of recognition and income. In this sense, people who decide to become artists are extremely risk-loving; with few exceptions they are disappointed by not reaching the sphere of superstars. Some artists adjust by consciously producing for a local, rather isolated market. If they are lucky, they can survive but will never achieve great renown.

4.7 Creativity

Creativity is an essential aspect of the arts, at least in Western-dominated cultures. To become successful, a writer, composer, or painter must produce new ideas and concepts. The same increasingly applies to theatres, opera houses, and festivals, which must distinguish themselves by being different from other performing arts organizations.

Two types of creativity can be distinguished.

4.7.1 Personal Creativity

This creativity is based on the intrinsic motivation to be artistically innovative. Intrinsically motivated individuals pursue artistic activities for their own sake. Personal creativity is a feature of the individual's motivations.

- *Intrinsic creativity*
  The dominant view held by art historians, art experts, and artists themselves is that only intrinsically motivated individuals can produce creative art. An artist who is paid, whether by public subsidies or the market, is discouraged from spending time on unpaid activities, even though these might result in innovations. The time-consuming creative activity is then reduced in favour of producing tried-and-tested work for the artistic market. This rising opportunity cost of time particularly affects artists who are successful in the market. In contrast, young artists with low opportunity cost can afford to spend more time on potentially creative activities. This opportunity-cost argument helps to explain why young artists are often more creative than older artists. There are fewer commercially failing older artists than younger artists, because unsuccessful artists tend to take up better-paid occupations.

- *Extrinsically induced creativity*
  Artists are thought to be more creative when the benefits of being so are higher and the costs are lower. In particular, when the government subsidizes artists, it becomes more profitable to work as an artist, so creativity is increased. The same effect occurs when artists can easily earn more money by selling their art on the market. If actors in a market are indeed able to recognize creativity, and if there is a demand for artistic creativity, innovative art reaches higher prices, and artists have an incentive to produce such art.
  When external rewards are available, highly motivated individuals may reduce their intrinsic motivation. The introduction of an external incentive means that intrinsic motivation is no longer needed or appreciated. This relationship is known as the crowding-out effect. It occurs when the external intervention is perceived to be controlling. These crowding-out effects comprise a new aspect of economic theory. They are the opposite of the relative price effect: an increase in price or monetary rewards decreases effort and creativity. To become successful, a writer, composer or painter must produce creative ideas and concepts.

4.7.2 Institutional Creativity

This is the creativity produced by suitable institutional conditions. One institution that particularly supports creativity is the price system. This also applies to the art market. Prices produce incentives to be innovative, provided there is a corresponding demand, and reward those who are successful in this endeavour.

The negative effects of some types of institutions on creativity have also been well studied in art economics. For example, guaranteed public financing of the budget deficits of cultural organizations, prevalent in many European countries, discourages creativity. Receiving funds largely independent of performance makes for a comfortable life, but it promotes conservatism rather than creativity. The recipients have an overwhelming urge to remain with the easy source of finance. Accordingly, they have a strong interest in not antagonizing the politicians and bureaucrats who hand out the money by producing innovative art, which often fosters conflict. The many government regulations and restrictions imposed on public art institutions are another constraint on creativity, as they hamper or forbid change. The same holds true for union restrictions. Orchestras, theatres, and opera houses often have unconventional working hours, which tend to conflict with rigid union rules. Modern governments have increasingly stepped in with direct and indirect subsidies, which have been accompanied by ever-increasing regulations. As a result, recipients are at risk of becoming fossilized and have partly succumbed to that danger.

Interestingly enough, institutions that damage creativity may indirectly promote artistic innovation elsewhere. Individuals with strong intrinsic motivation to be artistically innovative (i.e. having high personal creativity) will seek ways to fulfil this desire outside the established art that is manipulated by public intervention.

4.8 Are Artists Really Unhappy?

Careful empirical research finds that artists are considerably more satisfied with their work than non-artists. Their happiness can be attributed to the nature of artistic work. Artists have a high rate of self-employment, and self-employed individuals in any field are more likely to report higher satisfaction in their work. The reason is that they are to some extent autonomous and can undertake their work according to their own preferences and ideas.

Another important reason for artists' happiness lies in the process of artistic work, which includes variety and the opportunity to experience and learn new things. While income affects job satisfaction for both artists and non-artists, the effect is substantially smaller for artists. Quite unlike other professions, artists report higher job satisfaction with more working hours. However, it might be that causality runs in the opposite direction, namely that more satisfied people become artists, or that the increased satisfaction of artists is due to ingrained personality traits rather than the effects of the work. Nevertheless, considerable evidence indicates that artists are happier with their work than are people in other professions.

4.9 Conclusion

Artists receive on average lower income than other people of similar age, the same gender, and the same number of years of education. A few very successful superstars earn high incomes. One major reason for this is that there are many winner-take-all markets in the cultural sector. This leads to substantial inequality among artists. Care must be taken not to try to equalize incomes. To become successful, a writer, composer, or painter must produce creative ideas and concepts. Artists with high incomes do not necessarily produce bad art. Indeed, they are often among the best artists.

The best way to support the artistic professions is to improve the basic conditions under which they work. Talent is not enough. A fruitful approach is to support good schools of art in order to help would-be artists to establish contacts in the art world and to propagate their artistic output. Due to the strong external effects of culture not captured by markets, the public sector supports cultural activities by direct and indirect subsidies. As a result, the position of artists in the labour market is improved, raising incomes and employment opportunities. An attractive feature of this market is that artists are more satisfied with their work than non-artists, mainly because they are intrinsically motivated and enjoy an extent of autonomy.

Related Literature

A basic contribution to artists' labour markets is

Throsby D (2001) Economics and culture. Cambridge University Press, Cambridge

Major insights into the unequal distribution of income among artists include

Frank RH, Cook PJ (1995) The winner-take-all-society: why the few at the top get so much more than the rest of us. Free Press, New York
Rosen S (1981) The economics of superstars. Am Econ Rev 71(5):845–858

Awards are discussed in

Frey BS, Gallus J (2017) Honours versus money. The economics of awards. Oxford University Press, Oxford

Artists' happiness is empirically analysed in

Trine B, Fjællegaard CB, Frey BS, Steiner L (2013) Happiness in the arts—international evidence on artists' job satisfaction. Econ Lett 121(1):15–18
Steiner L, Schneider L (2013) The happy artist: an empirical application of the work-preference model. J Cult Econ 37(2):225–246

A general discussion of happiness research is given in

Frey BS (2018) Economics of happiness. SpringerBriefs in Economics, Springer International Publishing, Cham

Chapter 5
Reproductions in Art

Abstract The economic approach to art and culture takes a rather positive attitude towards copies, reproductions, and fakes. In contrast, the art-historical view tends to regard them in a negative way. The multiplication of the original creates utility for individuals demanding and paying for replicas. However, forgeries do create some problems. Significant costs are created on both the demand and supply sides of a market by both originals and copies. But many such problems can be mitigated or even overcome by appropriate legal constructs and institutional arrangements.

Keywords Copies · Reproductions · Fakes · Forgeries · Moral view · Legal view · Originals · Art history · Recognition

5.1 Contrasting Views on Copies and Fakes

5.1.1 The Moral View

The sense that copying art works is wrong has changed strongly over time. In former centuries in the West, and even more elsewhere, replicating the work of other artists was a perfectly acceptable activity. Michelangelo reproduced a work by his master Domenico Ghirlandaio in order to demonstrate his ability as an artist. There are even accounts of purchasers who welcomed a reproduction, even though they had bought it as an original.

In modern times, some artists, such as Salvador Dalí and René Magritte, have intentionally erased the difference between original and fake in order to revolt against the burden of the dead past. Obviously, if these artists, and movements such as performance art, auto-destructive art, and earth art, refuse to make the distinction, there is neither a moral nor legal case against "fakes"—the term loses its meaning.

B. S. Frey, *Economics of Art and Culture*, SpringerBriefs in Economics,
https://doi.org/10.1007/978-3-030-15748-7_5

5.1.2 The Legal View

Lawyers tend to look at fakes in terms of forgery and counterfeiting; fraud should therefore be prohibited. They are concerned with fraud linked with the production, sale, and purchase of reproductions. Two situations are prominent.

Firstly, a person buys a fake assuming it to be an original. He or she has acquired a work of art and can have reasonable expectations that it meets the conditions under which it has been sold. Thus, a painting bought from a well-established art dealer or in bidding performed in a respectable auction house should indeed be an original. Most auction houses guarantee that if the painting does not turn out to be an original as specified, it can be returned. However, in other cases where the seller deliberately cheats the buyer, the transaction constitutes an illegal act.

Secondly, an artist creates a tangible work such as a painting or sculpture or an intangible one such as a novel, play, or piece of music, but steals the idea from another artist without consent or compensation.

5.1.3 The Art Historic View

The dominant position in art history is that the original has a special and unique quality that fakes lack. The original oeuvre has an "aura" which, though invisible, is nevertheless taken to be real. In many cases, it is no longer possible for a viewer to distinguish the original from a reproduction; not even sophisticated technical means are always able to differentiate them. It is therefore the context and history of the original's creation which marks it as such and not its physical or aesthetic aspects. Yet the difference *is* real in the sense that most owners of art works are terribly disappointed when they detect that a presumed original piece is a copy. Nevertheless, it should be noted that this "cult of the original" is historically dependent. Vasari actually considered Michelangelo's copy of a statue by Ghirlandaio a triumph and this established the young Michelangelo among the great sculptors.

In contrast, Van Meegeren's copies of Vermeer were considered much inferior, but only once they were detected. The German artist Beltracchi became famous because he did not copy famous artists. Instead, he used their painting styles to create new works of art. He was imprisoned because he signed the new paintings with the names of the original artists. He no longer does so but develops as an artist in his own right. Many consider him to be a genius because he has the great sensitivity to paint works that famous artists could have painted but did not.

Partly due to these developments, some art historians take a more sanguine view of reproductions and fakes and no longer consider the aura to be attached only to the original. Instead, works of art are taken to be part of history, including their modifications, renovations, and copying.

5.2 Beneficial Aspects of Imitations

An economic point of view identifies three major benefits of copying.

5.2.1 Copies Provide Utility

The fact that an original is imitated and reproduced indicates that it is in demand. Consumers experience a benefit from viewing, reading, or hearing a work of art, which is reflected in their willingness to pay for it. Imitations serve to propagate the original to a wider audience, and so raise the total utility for prospective consumers. Owners of original artworks, among them most leading art museums, have started to sell exact replicas of selected pieces of their collections. This propagation effect also occurs when copies are made illegally. Some museums even deliberately mix copies with originals.

The creator of the original work of art may benefit from such imitations in two ways:

- He or she may receive royalties from legal copying. In the case of music, this is usually the artist's major source of income. It is of lesser importance for paintings, though in some cases the income gained is substantial.
- Even if copying is done without the consent of the creator of the original (i.e. illegally), he or she may nevertheless benefit indirectly from it. The creator's name is propagated, thus allowing him or her to sell future original works at higher prices.

The extent to which the propagation effect benefits the creator of the original depends on the specific conditions of an art market and the extent to which the copies effectively signal the original and its creator.

5.2.2 Artistic Capital Is Promoted

To produce faithful copies of great works has always been one of the major ways in which artists train themselves. This applies not only to lesser-known artists but also to painters who became great masters later in their lives. In addition, the existence of fakes presents a continuous challenge for art experts.

5.2.3 Supporting Creativity

The smaller the barriers against imitating, the greater is the scope for future artists to experiment. If the creator of the original can easily interfere by legal injunction, artistic creativity is hampered. Few great artists have not borrowed from earlier masters, and some of them have done so extensively—such as van Gogh or Dalí—and this has benefitted the arts.

The distinction between originals and copies is blurred. The term *original* is often poorly defined, and there is a continuous history in which copies, reproductions, and renovations play a role. Art does not end with the creation of the "original". A case in point may be Michelangelo's paintings in the Cappella Sistina: it is open to serious discussion what the original is, and where. In any case, thorough cleaning revealed a "new" art work to contemporary art lovers and art experts alike. The distinction between the original and copy has been further blurred in the digital age, which has made it possible to produce identical pieces of art at low cost.

5.3 Harmful Aspects of Imitations

It is useful to distinguish between the demand and supply sides.

5.3.1 Demand Side

Fakes present buyers with greater uncertainty about works of art they intend to purchase. There is a constant race between forgers and investigators. Both use increasingly sophisticated technical means. There are periods in which one side seems to prevail, but the incentives both to forge originals and to detect fakes is so strong that it can safely be predicted that neither side can win a permanent victory.

The uncertainty induced by the existence of fakes imposes costs on financial investors looking for high monetary returns from buying art. Provided that the indirect effect of propagation is small, they suffer a loss from the manufacture of copies and, of course, from buying a piece of work that is presumed to be original. However, such loss is smaller than it seems at first. Reasonably informed buyers are well aware of both problems and are therefore prepared to pay a correspondingly lower price for the artwork.

Uncertainty due to fakes does create real resource costs in the form of outlays of time, effort and money for search and information activities. As economic theory predicts, these costs create incentives to mitigate them:

- There are specialized suppliers who can be trusted, because they would otherwise lose their reputation and future business. There is a niche for serious art dealers, galleries and auction houses.
- Legal rules exist which allow hedging against various degrees of uncertainty.

In both cases, higher certainty about the artwork is reflected in higher purchase prices. There is thus a trade-off between risk and price, thus allowing prospective buyers to choose a particular degree of certainty. It is wrong to think that buyers are solely the passive victims of forgers; they can react actively to the possibility of fakes.

5.3.2 *Supply Side*

Fakes affect the incentive to produce original art. There is a trade-off. Free imitation of originals produces utility for consumers, but at the same time reduces the direct profitability of innovations to producers. Most legal systems strike a balance by granting innovators a monopoly for a restricted period of time. This also applies to some, but not all, artistic originals.

An essential question is the extent to which artistic creativity depends on monetary incentives. Considerable empirical evidence indicates that intrinsic motivation is crucial for artists' personal creativity. Artists may be strongly interested in monetary income, but at least at the start of their careers—the period when they are generally most creative and innovative—they are primarily driven by intrinsic motivation, perhaps even by a strong drive to embark on artistic endeavours. Only at a later stage in an artist's life does monetary income beyond what is needed for subsistence seem to become more important or predominant.

5.4 What to Do?

The discussion suggests that the beneficial aspects of fakes are rather strong and the harmful effects rather weak. Copying is a response to demand from people who are otherwise unable to enjoy an original work of art. *Once produced*, the work should be offered at zero price to the public. The consumption of a copy produces utility, and should therefore not be curtailed or prohibited. Moreover, faking benefits the originator when it provides additional recognition and fame. The harmful effect of faking, raising uncertainty for prospective buyers, is reduced or even eliminated by the development of legal guarantees. Buying from reputable art dealers and auctioneers also reduces uncertainty.

Faking art has some harmful effects. A repressive approach that tolerates copying only with the explicit consent of the creator and in which all other reproductions are automatically considered forgeries imposes significant burdens on society. Two types of costs can be differentiated:

- Considerable energy and material resources are wasted in fighting over which artist should have the property right for the original, and who copied from whom. Another issue to be settled is how far the monopoly right should extend. If it is defined too extensively, artistic progress is hampered, because an artist must seek the approval of the owner of the property before he or she works in this direction. The flow of creative artistic activity is reduced.
- The repressive policy against copying produces its own costs for art lawyers and the judiciary. Copying tends to move underground. Organized crime is favoured.

A repressive policy against fakes makes little sense. The creator of an original piece of art should indeed be given an incentive to pursue his or her activity, but this incentive need not be given by granting a monopoly right. In the world of art, recognition plays a central role. The prospect of becoming famous is certainly a strong incentive to be creative. A good solution that balances the benefits and costs discussed would be to force every copier to explicitly acknowledge his or her sources of inspiration. It provides recognition for art creators, but no direct monetary payments are involved. The recognition received generates reputation and fame, which can then be transformed into higher monetary income by better job offers, popular publications, and well-paid talks. Once this acknowledgement has been made, the process of copying, imitating, faking, or forging may run its course: the distinction between these terms becomes immaterial.

The suggestion of "art quotations" remains valid in the digital age. It corresponds to the need to compensate the creator of an original work of art at the very beginning, because imitations simply cannot be prevented.

5.5 Conclusion

The economic approach to art and culture considers copies, reproductions, and fakes as providing utility for the consumers demanding, and paying, for them. However, significant costs are involved. On the demand side, uncertainty about art works is increased. This cost can at least partly be overcome by resorting to knowledgeable and reputable sellers of art. Legal rules also help to reduce prospective buyers' uncertainty and possible losses.

On the supply side, creators of original pieces of art must be given an incentive to pursue their activities. Recognition plays a central role. The prospect of becoming famous is certainly a strong incentive to be creative. A good solution that balances the benefits and costs discussed would be to legally force copiers to explicitly acknowledge their sources of inspiration.

Related Literature

General accounts of copies, reproductions, and fakes in the arts are provided in

Dutton D (1983) The forger's art: forgery and the philosophy of art. University of California Press, Berkeley

Hamilton C (1980) Great forgers and famous fakes: the manuscript forgers of America and how they duped the experts. Crown Publishers, New York

Jones M (ed) (1990) Fake? The art of deception. British Museum Press, London

Economic analyses are provided by

Benhamou F, Ginsburgh V (1998) Is there a market for copies? In: Mossetto G, Vecco M (eds) The economics of copying and counterfeiting. Franco Angeli, Milano
Deardorff AV (1995) The appropriate extent of intellectual property rights in art. J Cult Econ 19(2):119–130
Greffe X (1998) Intellectual property right in the digital age. In: Mossetto G, Vecco M (eds) The economics of copying and counterfeiting. Franco Angeli, Milano
Hansman H, Santilli M (1997) Authors' and artists' moral rights: a comparative legal and economic analysis. J Legal Stud 26(2):95–143
Koboldt C (1995) Intellectual property and optimal copyright protection. J Cult Econ 19(2):131–155
Pommerehne WW, Granica MJ (1995) Perfect reproduction of works of art: substitutes or heresy? J Cult Econ 19(3):237–249

Part III
Areas

Chapter 6
Creative Cultural Economy

Abstract Industries combining creative cultural work and commerce today constitute a well-organized part of the economy. The creative cultural economy is characterized by high entry cost, great uncertainty, and strongly knowledge-based and labour-intensive production. It uses advanced, often digitized technology. Technological change may lead to lock-in effects. As a consequence, switching from an older to a newer technology may incur significant costs.

Keywords Cultural work · Creativity · Commerce · Knowledge-intensive · Labour-intensive · Digitized technology · Entry cost

6.1 Creativity and Culture

Industries combining creative cultural work and commerce foster a rapidly growing sector of modern society. While art and culture have always been closely connected with the economy, the creative cultural industries today constitute a well-organized and commercialized part of the economy.

Cultural creative industries are closely related to the information, digital, and internet industries; they fully exploit the new communication technologies in global markets.

Creative industries exist in the following areas:

- Most importantly in the arts in the narrow sense:

  Performing arts, comprising theatre, opera, dance;
  Visual arts, comprising painting, drawing, sculpture, ceramics, photography;
  Music;
  Literature.

- In the arts in a broader sense:

  Museums devoted to art, history, archaeology, the military, science, technology, transport, and many other subjects;
  Libraries and archives;

B. S. Frey, *Economics of Art and Culture*, SpringerBriefs in Economics,
https://doi.org/10.1007/978-3-030-15748-7_6

Built, movable, and intangible heritage.

- The media:

  Television, radio, broadcasting, video, computer software and games; Publishing and printing.

- Related areas:

  Architecture, crafts, design, fashion, and advertising.

These industries contribute increasingly to the level and growth of the economy, to employment, and to international trade.

6.2 Economic Properties

Three main aspects characterize the creative cultural economy:

- High barriers to entry due to high fixed costs. Additional consumers can be served at low, and sometimes close to zero, marginal cost. These increasing economies of scale make entry into the markets difficult because copyrights, patents, and trademarks protect the intellectual property created. They are imposed in order to economically stimulate the provision of new cultural objects.
- Supply is faced with high great uncertainty as it is difficult, and in many cases impossible, to predict how potential consumers will receive a newly created cultural product. This uncertainty tends to be even larger than in other sectors of the economy.
- Production is highly knowledge based, labour intensive, and often uses advanced technology. Digitization plays a large role. Technological change may lead to lock-in effects. As a consequence, switching from an older to a newer technology may incur significant costs.

Many different types of contracts determine the terms of transactions in the creative economy. Contracts may be implicit and informal, as for instance is the case between an artist painter and a gallery. The latter takes paintings by the artist, exhibits them, and sells them at a commission. A contract may also be relational; the partners involved create a transaction-specific asset, which would otherwise not be produced. Contracts may also specify incentives to produce, to advertise, and to sell. An option contract allows entrepreneurs to assess the marketability of an art work before they undertake further investments. In the case of a film, for instance, the entrepreneur pays the often-high production costs but afterwards is free to decide whether to proceed at all, or how many resources to put into advertising and releasing the film.

6.3 Conclusion

Cultural industries are an important and rapidly growing sector of the economy. They differ markedly from classical industry due to more extensive economies of scale, greater uncertainty, and a larger proportion of highly educated employees. These characteristics favour the emergence of oligopolies or even monopolies. As a consequence, market forces can be undermined, leaving consumers confronted with limited choice and high prices. The public sector must take care to prevent such unfavourable outcomes by pursuing anti-monopoly policies. In addition, great efforts must be made to keep the cultural industry open to newcomers.

Related Literature

Important contributions to the creative economy include

Towse R (2001) Creativity, incentive and reward. An economic analysis of copyright and culture in the information age. Edward Elgar, Cheltenham UK and Northampton, MA. USA

Throsby D (2001) Economics and culture. Cambridge University Press, Cambridge

Many topics are treated in the following collection of articles

Towse R, Handke C (eds) (2013) Handbook on the digital creative economy. Edward Elgar, Cheltenham UK and Northampton, MA. USA

Contracts in the creative economy are analysed in

Caves RE (2000) Creative industries: contracts between art and commerce. Harvard University Press, Cambridge MA

Chapter 7
The Performing Arts

Abstract Only a small proportion of the population ever attends live performances of classical art. Crucial determinants are entry price, education, and preferences. The public sector can support the performing arts by giving a fixed sum, by making donations tax deductible, and by covering the deficit. Profit-oriented firms can exist when fixed costs are small, audiences large, and price discrimination and cross-subsidization feasible. There may also be co-operatives. The cost disease threatens the survival of the performing arts because the wages paid must rise in line with the other sectors in the economy. Labour productivity often cannot be raised. Admission prices can be increased provided consumer react little to price changes. Artistic performances can be made more attractive to a larger proportion of people.

Keywords Live performance · Classical art · Public sector · Profit-oriented firms · Co-operatives · Fixed cost · Audiences · Admission prices · Price discrimination · Education · Cost disease · Labour productivity · Deficits · Opera houses · Opera composers · Opera plays · Drama · Playwright · Government support · Subsidy · Donations · Taxes

7.1 Characteristics of the Performing Art

The live performing arts comprise opera, theatre, dance and orchestra. In each case there are classical forms—operas by Verdi, plays by Shakespeare, and symphonies by Beethoven—as well as more popular forms such as open-air pop concerts. Common to all live performances is their presentation at given points of time, after which they disappear. The resources to be supplied are largely independent of the size of the audience. For instance, it is impossible to reduce the length of an opera because not all seats are occupied.

B. S. Frey, *Economics of Art and Culture*, SpringerBriefs in Economics,
https://doi.org/10.1007/978-3-030-15748-7_7

7.2 Demand Side

Only a small proportion of the population ever attends a live performance in classical art. In contrast, many art lovers attend such performances repeatedly and form a kind of supporting group.

An important determinant of attendance is price. This consists of the entry price determined by the performing organization, the cost of transport, parking fees, dressing up as necessary, and of securing a ticket. The opportunities to spend the time with other activities are also highly relevant. It often seems to be more comfortable to spend an evening watching TV than to incur the effort of attending an evening at the opera.

People with higher income are much more likely to attend the classical performing arts than are low-income recipients. This is obviously because the entry prices to the venues are often substantial.

Education determines participation in the classical performing arts to a large extent. People who attended high school or universities are better endowed to enjoy this kind of art. They have often been taught from early childhood about the pleasure to be gained from attending such performances. This effect is bolstered when individuals' education correlates strongly with their parents'. Indeed, most adherents of opera, theatre, dance, and classical music have been encouraged by their parents.

Independent of income and education, some people greatly enjoy classic live performances. This applies in particular to groups of young people with low income and incomplete education who are fond of these artistic activities, for instance classical ballet.

7.3 Supply Side

The performing arts are characterized by high fixed costs. These are constant costs arising independent of the number of performances or the size of the audience. In order to present a theatrical play, all the actors and the supporting technical and administrative staff must be present; the cast can hardly be reduced because the audience is small.

7.3.1 Operas

Table 7.1 presents a list of some of the leading opera houses of the world.

The list presented in Table 7.1 is quite limited and not based on attendance numbers because this depends strongly on the size of an opera house. Rather, the selection is based on which opera houses are best known, especially to tourists visiting a city.

Table 7.1 Famous opera houses

La Scala	Milan
Teatro di San Carlo	Naples
Paris Opéra	Paris
Opéra Royale	Versailles
Wiener Staatsoper	Vienna
The Royal Opera House at Covent Garden	London
The Bolshoi	Moscow
Teatro Colon	Buenos Aires
Sidney Opera House	Sydney
Metropolitan Opera	New York

Table 7.2 The ten most often played opera composers according to performances over the seasons 2013/14 to 2017/18

Composer	Performances
Giuseppe Verdi	16,122
Wolfgang Amadeus Mozart	11,887
Giacomo Puccini	11,615
Gioachino Rossini	5237
Gaetano Donizetti	4691
Richard Wagner	4093
George Bizet	4027
Johann Strauss	2863
Pyotr Ilych Tschaikovsky	2709
Richard Strauss	2319

Source Opera Statistics 2017/18

Even well-known opera houses such as Il Teatro La Fenice in Venice and The Semper Oper in Dresden are not listed.

Seven of the opera houses considered top according to Table 7.1 are located in Europe, and only one each in South America, North America, and Australia. Among the European ones, some have a long history. The Covent Garden was opened in 1732, the Opera in Naples in 1737, the one in Versailles in 1769, and the Scala in 1778.

The cities with most opera performances in the 2015/16 season are Moscow with 582 performances, Vienna with 535, Berlin with 527, London with 427, and St. Petersburg with 422. This list again reflects the dominance of European opera houses (Opera Statistics 2017/18).

Table 7.2 lists the most often played opera composers.

The most dominant by far are Verdi, Mozart, and Puccini. Four of the ten most frequently performed composers are Italian (Verdi, Puccini, Rossini, and Donizetti), two are Austrian (Mozart and Johann Strauss), two are German (Wagner and Richard

Table 7.3 The ten most performed opera plays over the seasons 2013/14 to 2017/18 all over the world

Play	Composer
La Traviata	Verdi
Carmen	Bizet
Die Zauberflöte	Mozart
La Bohème	Puccini
Tosca	Puccini
Le Nozze di Figaro	Mozart
Madame Butterfly	Puccini
Il Barbiere di Siviglia	Rossini
Rigoletto	Verdi
Don Giovanni	Mozart

Source Opera Statistics 2017/18

Strauss), one is French (Bizet), and one is Russian (Tchaikovsky). This is an extreme concentration in only a few countries of the world.

The composers most often performed mostly lived in the 18th and 19th centuries. Living composers lag far behind. The leading ones, Glass, Heggie, Dove, Evers and Adès, are little known to the general public and can muster only between 132 and 321 performances, compared to the 11,000 to 16,000 performances of the most popular, Verdi, Mozart, and Puccini.

Table 7.3 shows the most popular operas. Again, these were written in the 18th and 19th centuries.

Here again the Italians dominate by far. The only three operas by composers of other countries are those by Bizet and Mozart. The latter is the most represented composer, with *Die Zauberflöte*, *Le Nozze di Figaro*, and *Don Giovanni*.

7.3.2 Drama

Many famous theatres all over the world are often also visited by cultural tourists. It suffices to mention the ancient Greek and Roman theatres such as those in Delphi and Ephesus (4th Century BC), Amman and Taormina (2nd Century BC), and the theatres on Athen's Acropolis, in Orange, and in Ephesus (1st Century AD). And there are theatres such as the Comédie Française in Paris and the Burgtheater in Vienna.

Table 7.4 provides a list of the most popular dramas performed in German theatres.

Though Table 7.4 refers to plays presented in German theatres, the most popular are not necessarily by German authors. Shakespeare is represented by no fewer than four plays among the top ten. Indeed, he is considered part of the German theatrical tradition thanks to the early circulation of excellent translations.

Table 7.4 Most performed dramas in Germany, 1990–2002

Play	Year of first performance	Playwright
Die Dreigroschenoper	1928	Berthold Brecht
Ein Sommernachtstraum	About 1595	William Shakespeare
Romeo and Julia	About 1595	William Shakespeare
Nathan der Weise	1783	Gotthold Ephraim Lessing
Faust I	1829	Johann Wolfgang von Goethe
Der zerbrochene Krug	1808	Heinrich von Kleist
Was ihr wollt	1600	William Shakespeare
Kabale und Liebe	1784	Friedrich Schiller
Hamlet	1601	William Shakespeare
Maria Stuart	1800	Friedrich Schiller

Source FOCUS Magazin 38 (2003), based on Werkstatistik des Deutschen Bühnenvereins

Only one of the plays, Brecht's *Dreigroschenoper*, was written in the 20th century while the others date from the end of the 16th to the very beginning of the 19th centuries.

Various types of organizations are active in the supply of the performing arts. They differ in their behaviour depending on the institutional conditions and the incentives provided.

7.3.3 Government Supported Organizations

Most opera houses, theatres, ballet companies, and orchestras today are to a large extent financed by the public. On the European continent, government plays a dominant role. In Germany, for instance, the government pays 80% or more of the costs. The way public support is given has a strong influence on the quantity and quality of art performed as well as on the admission prices charged.

These are the most important forms of public support:

- A *fixed sum* of money is given depending solely on the fact that an organization exists to supply this kind of art. Such lump-sum support helps the suppliers to survive, at least in the short run; they would otherwise have to close down for financial reasons. A fixed subsidy induces the managers of the receiving organizations to avoid any profits, because if they declare that they earn net revenues, the subsidy will be reduced or discontinued altogether. Instead, it is important to show to the public officials in charge that they urgently need the public funds. This mechanism gives the managers an incentive to produce performances of particularly high quality and to pay the artists and the supporting staff more than they can earn elsewhere.

- *Tax deductibility of donations* by individuals and corporate sponsors. The latter can also declare such expenditures as part of their marketing effort and thus as non-taxable cost. These tax expenditures play a large role in the United States, where about half the contributions to charities and to performing arts organizations is tax exempt. The corresponding tax deductions are generally much lower in Europe and elsewhere.
- Again, the managers of performing arts venues have an incentive to avoid profits by charging low entry prices as this is considered to be socially beneficial behaviour. Much effort is expended to attract donors and sponsors, sometimes allowing them to intervene in the artistic activities. Corporations may, for instance, dislike theatrical plays attacking the capitalist system or firms like themselves, in which case they may try to convince the management to choose other plays—and are often successful, because the theatres need the financial support of corporations. Private donors are attracted by enhancing their prestige, in particular by obtaining nice titles such as patron, benefactor, or contributor, and by publicizing these contributions wherever possible.
- *Deficit coverage*. In many countries, this is the most popular form of support for the performing arts. On the European continent, many organizations are even part of the public administration and are closely tied to the way in which the administration runs the budget. Many items of expenditure may not be substituted for each other or over time. Such regulations reduce the scope of managers and artistic directors to run the organization as they see fit.
- The subsidy is determined on the basis of the projected deficit. This is often done yearly; only recently have governments turned to longer-run subsidy schemes. This gives the management more flexibility; they need not, for instance, exaggerate their expenditures at the end of the year to avoid having their subsidy reduced in the next year. Nevertheless, the managers have an incentive to increase costs in order not to lose deficit coverage. They are always able to argue that artistic quality can only be maintained if the size of the subsidy is maintained or increased. The public officials and politicians in charge have little motivated to demonstrate that some items of expenditure could be reduced. Compared to the people running the performing arts organizations, they lack competence and information, a fact that has often been exploited by the subsidy recipients. As a consequence, performing arts managers who profit from a well-established deficit coverage scheme have few incentives to reduce their fixed costs or to undertake measures to raise revenue.

7.3.4 Profit-Oriented Enterprises

It is difficult to run a firm in the performing arts if it depends on making a profit. However, some conditions favour private, profit-making enterprises:

- When set-up and fixed costs are small. This may be the case for newly formed enterprises catering for a specialist audience, say a particular type of modern ballet.

- When audiences are large and prepared to pay the often-high admission prices. This is rarely the case for the classical performing arts but may be so for venues offering more popular performances, such as musicals. On Broadway, *The King and I*, *My Fair Lady*, *Oklahoma!*, and *West Side Story* have been great successes, followed more recently by musicals such as the *Phantom of the Opera*, *Les Misérables*, and *Beauty and the Beast*. This may also, but less often, occur for plays. Examples include *Arsenic and Old Lace*, *Amadeus*, *Dracula*, and even more serious performances such as *Hamlet*, *A Streetcar Named Desire*, and *Cat on a Hot Tin Roof*.
- When price discrimination is feasible. Different prices for different categories of consumer—for instance the young and the old, for handicapped people, for students and other selected professions, for nationals and tourists—can be introduced only if these groups can be neatly separated. Otherwise, too many people will exploit the low prices. Price discrimination may also apply to the time of day (they may be lower for the afternoon than for the evening) and to the season (higher in summer than in winter).
- When cross-subsidization is possible with highly profitable other attractions. An example is Las Vegas and other casino resorts. People spend huge sums playing roulette, blackjack, and other games, producing high profits for the casinos. But they are also attracted by popular art performances, including circuses such as the Cirque du Soleil.

7.3.5 Co-operative Organizations

In the performing arts, the artists, who are the labour, hire capital; this is the reverse of what happens in the other sectors of the economy, where capital hires labour. One example is a group of actors who want to perform one or several plays and look for capital to meet the expenditure. Such groups are often informal, and the management tasks are shared. Under these circumstances, joint production by a team is effective. The problems of monitoring effort and remuneration are solved by common high intrinsic motivation and mutual control. As long as such a co-operative venture is small, it may exist for a considerable period.

When a co-operative artistic group becomes successful, various problems arise. The remuneration can no longer be amicably determined but depends on the importance of the task. The artistic, technical, and administrative roles become increasingly separated, and a more hierarchical set-up evolves. A division can emerge between those who directly reap the artistic success of the production and those who do the less visible auxiliary, backstage and administrative work. They must be compensated in some form, often by higher wages. This often means that the co-operative form of organization is relinquished.

7.3.6 The Cost Disease

The performing arts find themselves in a difficult situation in which it is hard to exist without outside subsidies. This is for three reasons:

- Highly qualified labour is a dominant cost factor. The performing arts are part of the service sector of the economy, where labour is more important than in industry and modern agriculture. The wages to be paid constitute a large part of the total expenditures.
- The wages to be paid in the arts sector develop more or less in line with other wages in the economy. Per capita economic growth is mainly a result of increases in labour productivity, which leads to continually rising average wages. As a result, there is a constant demand to also raise salaries in the performing arts.
- It is difficult, and in some instances impossible, to raise labour productivity in the performing arts. A symphony by Mozart cannot be played at double speed or with only half the musicians.

This cost disease in the performing arts is not an immutable law. There are various ways in which its effects can be mitigated:

- Admission prices can be raised to meet the higher cost of labour. As labour costs keep growing, prices must be continually increased. Whether a price rise leads to higher revenue depends on the elasticity of demand. If many would-be consumers decide to no longer attend, revenue falls. Empirical research suggests that the price elasticity of demand is smaller than minus one. In other words, a price rise does yield higher revenue. But it is doubtful whether this holds in the long run when attendance prices continually increase.
- Efforts can be expended to increase the productivity of performing arts activities. This is possible in the technical sector, where electronics and digitization enable more efficient production.
- The artistic realm also exhibits some restricted possibilities to raise productivity. It has been observed that some theatres choose plays requiring only a small cast, and authors may respond by writing plays with fewer actors. Even Shakespeare's plays have been produced with fewer actors by reducing the size of the crowds appearing. The question, of course, is whether this makes sense or destroys the artistic value of the work.
- Demand can be raised by combining the performance of operas, plays, dance exhibitions, and musical performances with an event, thereby making them more attractive to a wider set of people. An example is the museum nights in which the same collection as always is presented but in which a large crowd assembles that favours personal communication.

7.4 Conclusion

The performing arts are confronted with serious problems, in particular the cost disease. These financial problems can be overcome by government support. Other means include asking higher entry prices from consumers with higher willingness to pay by actively using price differentiation. The possibilities of raising labour productivity must be examined, especially by using digital technologies. New ideas are sorely needed. Under these conditions, for-profit and co-operative firms may survive.

Related Literature

Various aspects of the performing arts are competently treated in handbook articles by

Brooks AC (2006) Nonprofit firms in the performing arts. In: Ginsburgh VA, Throsby D (eds) Handbook of the economics of art and culture. Elsevier, Amsterdam, pp 473–506

Luksetich WA (2003) Orchestras. In: Towse R (ed) A handbook of cultural economics. Edward Elgar, Cheltenham UK and Northampton, MA, USA, pp 349–355

Schimmelpfennig J (2003) Ballet. In: Towse R (ed) A handbook of cultural economics. Edward Elgar, Cheltenham UK and Northampton, MA, USA, pp 85–90

Seaman BA (2006) Empirical studies of demand for the performing arts. In: Ginsburgh VA, Throsby D (eds) Handbook of the economics of art and culture. Elsevier, Amsterdam, pp 415–472

Towse R (2003) Opera. In: Towse R (ed) A handbook of cultural economics. Edward Elgar, Cheltenham UK and Northampton, MA, USA, pp 342–348

The cost disease was identified by

Baumol WJ, Bowen WG (1966) Performing arts. The economic dilemma; A study of problems common to theater, opera, music and dance. The Twentieth Century Fund, Hartford CT

Chapter 8
Festivals

Abstract Thousands of festivals take place every year, especially in the tourist season. The boom in music festivals poses a challenge to art economists because of the glaring contrast with the serious financial problems faced by theatres, opera houses, and orchestras with fixed venues. Festivals attract new groups of consumers. For tourists, attendance at festivals is a small proportion of total holiday expenditures, and demand people are not driven away by higher entry prices. Festivals benefit from the support of business which benefit from the media attention produced. They have lower production costs, offer more opportunities for artistic creativity, and are less restricted by regulations than are fixed venues. However, these advantages are unlikely to persist in the future.

Keywords Classical musical festivals · Consumers · Tourism · Holidays · Entry prices · Price elasticity · Media attention · Creativity · Fixed venues · Production cost · Union regulations · Government regulations · Popularization

8.1 An Abundance of Festivals

Virtually every city, or at least region, in Europe has its own musical or operatic festival. Today, many thousands of festivals take place each year.

Festivals became a significant part of the performing arts and of the serious music and opera scene in the 1920s, but the real boom has taken place within the last 30 years. When the European Festivals Association was founded in 1952, there were 15 festivals; in 2018 there were about 100 festivals, and the Association counts members in not less than 40 countries. The European Festival Association restricts its membership to the most prestigious festivals. Festivals usually take place in summer and are often very popular, particularly with tourists. Some festivals are permanently sold out, and entrance tickets can then only be acquired by good connections or on the black market. In the case of the Bayreuth Festival, which is mostly devoted to Wagner, ordinary visitors have to apply several times before they are able to purchase even a restricted number of tickets.

B. S. Frey, *Economics of Art and Culture*, SpringerBriefs in Economics,
https://doi.org/10.1007/978-3-030-15748-7_8

Table 8.1 Some leading classical music festivals

Salzburg Music Festival	Austria
Bayreuth Festival	Germany
Lucerne Summer Music Festival	Switzerland
Savonlinna Opera Festival	Finland
Verona Opera Festival	Italy
Glyndebourne Festival	England
Edinburgh International Festival	Scotland
Tanglewood Music Festival	USA
Hollywood Bowl	USA

Table 8.1 lists some of the best-known classical festivals.

8.2 A Paradox

The boom in music festivals poses a challenge to art economists because of the glaring contrast with the serious financial problems faced by theatres, opera houses and orchestras with a given venue. Many opera and concert houses are under such intense financial strain that they are forced to reduce their activities and dismiss artists, stage hands, and other employees or risk closing down completely. Unit labour costs of production in the live performing arts steadily increase because the wage rates in this sector rise at a rate similar to that in the economy as a whole, while labour productivity in the performing arts is more or less constant. This is the essence of the cost disease (see Chap. 7).

The basic idea of the cost disease provides a convincing explanation why live performing arts suppliers are in perennial financial difficulties and why many of them have not been able to survive. At the same time, musical festivals and special exhibitions are thriving. This is a surprising paradox, and one that calls for an explanation.

8.3 Features

8.3.1 *Demand Side*

The following features characterize festivals:

- *They are subject to a high-income effect.* Consumers tend to spend an increasing share of rising income on visiting musical performances. However, the same rising income presents people with higher opportunity costs of time, so they find it hard to attend the performing arts during the year. They find it increasingly difficult to devote a whole evening in order to attend an artistic event. In contrast, during the holiday period they have more time available, which makes a visit to a festival attractive. Thus, festivals find themselves in a growing market.

- *They attract new groups of visitors.* Many people are overawed by the "temples of culture", feel insecure and unwelcome, and therefore do not even consider attending an opera performance. This applies, in particular, to population groups with little formal education, and whose cultural traditions may only be sparsely retained. The situation clearly differs for special cultural events that are broadly advertised and that are made attractive to new groups. This holds in particular for music festivals taking place in public spaces. They are more amenable to the great mass of the population, and less imitating than the established temples of culture. Indeed, many festivals make a substantial effort to "go to the people", for instance by playing in sport stadiums or other popular meeting places such as inner-city parks.
- *Festivals focus attention.* A festival seeks to attract consumers by presenting an extraordinary cultural experience. They specialize in some particular artist (say Johann Sebastian Bach or Franz Schubert), some period (say renaissance music), some topic (say courtly music), some genre (say protest songs), or some type of presentation (say using original musical instruments). As a result, the visitors interested in such particular forms of art gather there, often from distant locations. This development is, of course, encouraged by low and falling travel costs. Public attention is drawn away from the regular performing art venues towards a special and unique, or at least rare, event. Attendance at festivals may even be compared to pilgrimages, which also have an aura of mysticism and are surrounded by much commercial activity.
- *Festivals are newsworthy.* Festivals are news and attract the attention of television, radio, and the print and digital media. A substantial advantage is that this media attention is free of charge. In contrast, regular operatic and musical performers attract at best some media attention on opening nights. With few exceptions, the subsequent reports are digested by only a small percentage of the population. Festivals offer much better opportunities to attract media attention because they present themselves every year as a special occasion. This holds true even if they continually repeat performances, as the Verona Festival does with "Aida".

  Closely connected to novelty is the limited duration of festivals. The restricted time raises prospective visitors' incentives to attend, while a visit to the local opera house or concert hall is easily postponed in the expectation that nothing is lost.
- *Attending festivals is relatively low cost.* Festivals are closely connected to tourism. The French characteristically name them *estivals* to indicate that they normally take place in the summer tourist season. As tourists on average benefit from constantly rising incomes, they increase their vacation expenditure and correspondingly demand more cultural experiences during their stay abroad. A considerable proportion of visitors to a typical festival come from out of town, from another region, and often from a foreign country.

The combination of a cultural event with tourism lowers individuals' cost of attending in various respects. In the case of the increasingly popular package tours, the consumers only have to take the initial decision, and all the rest is taken care of by the travel agent. In the case of festivals, for it is often burdensome to acquire tickets, this reduction in decision and transaction costs is substantial.

- *Price elasticity of demand for festivals is low*. The strong attraction of festivals to tourists and people from out of town on daytrips also affects the price elasticity of demand. Tourists tend to compare the ticket price to expenditures for the trip as a whole. A price rise then appears small and does not have much impact on demand. The low price elasticity of demand, compared to that of permanent venues, gives the managers of festivals more leeway to bolster their revenue by increasing entrance fees.

8.3.2 Supply Side

The supply of music festivals is determined by four major features. They contrast with the conditions faced by the permanent venues and contribute to the boom in festivals.

- *Production costs are relatively low*. The absolute cost of many festivals is certainly high, but it is low compared to the expenditures required if they had to meet all costs. Important resources are taken free of charge from the permanent venues. This applies in particular to the actors and singers who often are employed by a fixed venue which has to carry the substantial cost of health insurance and old age pensions. In contrast, a festival can hire artists during their holiday period without being burdened by these additional costs.

  As festivals are predominantly organized during the summer holidays, they can hire many of the artistic and technical staff at relatively low cost. They can also draw on volunteers to a considerable extent. The locations at which festivals play are often public—they belong to the state or the church—can be rented at a nominal charge, and are frequently free. This makes sense, as many of these venues are otherwise unused, for example the Roman theatres in which festivals such as Verona and Orange take place.
- *There is more scope for artistic creativity*. Permanent opera houses and orchestras are strongly bound by the clientele they have to cater for. They often find it impossible to interpret classical plays in a new form, and even more to perform modern and/or unknown plays, because they risk losing their regular customers. The holders of season tickets with mostly conservative taste are, moreover, strongly interested in what is presented and form a powerful lobby. They can thus exert considerable pressure on the managers and the subsidy-giving politicians if they are dissatisfied with "their" opera house or orchestras. As a consequence, the directors have little opportunity to fulfil their artistic conceptions of originality.

In contrast, independently organized festivals provide an opportunity for exhibiting artistic creativity. Festivals can readily specialize in an audience interested in unorthodoxy, excellence, and special tastes. A festival exclusively devoted to contemporary art may well prosper, as the festivals at Donaueschingen and Lockenhaus demonstrate.

- *Circumventing government and trade union regulations*. In continental Europe, establishments of classical orchestras and operas are to a large extent either directly part of the public administration or at least have to follow the administrative rules of the public sector as they are heavily subsidized by it. In particular, they are subject to the *non-affectation principle*, according to which all expenditures are covered by the public budget, and in return all the revenue goes to the public treasury. All revenue gained is "taxed" by the public treasury at one hundred per cent as the subsidy is correspondingly reduced. As a result, arts institutions are little motivated to increase their revenues by their own efforts.
  Government restrictions go far beyond budgetary affairs. They hinder the art institutions' way of acting and performing in a plethora of ways. Thus, pricing policy is very restricted, as are opening and performing days and hours. Festivals present a major chance to avoid these regulations. They are, with very few exceptions, organized as private enterprises, in which public bodies are at best one of several members. As a consequence, the directors of music festivals have to conform to less administrative regulations, and in particular do not have to transfer surpluses to the public treasury. Instead, they can use them in ways they find reasonable, above all by investing them in innovative features of their festival.
  One of the most stringent public regulations imposed on art institutions pertains to government sector employment. The virtual impossibility of dismissing inefficient or downright destructive employees, promoting and paying employees according to performance, and adjusting working hours to needs, are major factors that reduce creative endeavours and turn art institutions into mere bureaucracies. Additional regulations have been imposed by trade unions, and these are often fully supported by the government. Festivals and special exhibitions make it possible to evade at least some employment restrictions, especially as most festival employees are not union members but only part-time and temporary workers not legally bound by employment regulations.
- *Stronger public support*. Politicians and public officials have a pronounced interest in prominent festivals. Festivals not only respond to the demands of the arts world and the local business community but provide politicians with excellent opportunities for appearing in the media as "patrons of the arts" (with taxpayers' money). The fact that some festivals initially make a profit until politicians seize the chance to intervene suggests a causal effect opposite to the accepted one: subsidies are not offered because deficits must be covered, but deficits appear because politicians offer subsidies.
- *Business is more interested in supporting festivals*. Festivals offer many opportunities to make money. This feature applies not only to the tourist industry but also to firms catering for the production of festivals and exhibitions. There is also a benefit to the recording industry. CDs, videos, and digital representations of classi-

cal music have become a huge commercial enterprise, with correspondingly high profits. Festivals provide an excellent opportunity to hire superstars for often very large crowds of spectators. This effect is greatly magnified if the performances are televised and made available on the internet. The recording companies also use festivals to launch the careers of their future stars. As festivals are less regulated than concert and opera houses, these companies can more easily influence the programme to favour the artists they have under contract. The same applies to the sponsoring activity of companies producing goods unrelated to the arts. At festivals, they can appear more prominently and can therefore expect more publicity for a given sum of money.

Business is also more prepared to support festivals than regular activities, where legal provisions often hinder sponsoring. An important reason also is the higher media attention to these events. Corporate sponsors also feel that their contributions really add to cultural output and do not simply substitute for government subsidies.

Festivals are unlikely to draw visitors away from the performances of the established opera and orchestra companies. If anything, a glamorous and highly advertised festival raises people's interest in serious music and may even induce them to attend local art performances. As a side effect, festival visitors tend to entertain higher expectations concerning the quality of local performers. They may realize that these performers are sometimes far from top class, which tends to reduce attendance.

8.3.3 Possible Future Developments

Do all the advantages of festivals over local theatres, opera houses, dance and orchestras mean that festivals are going to dominate cultural events completely in the future? There are various reasons why this is not to be expected. Certainly, these special cultural events are here to stay, but they will become less special. As a result, the current gap between the traditional venues and festivals is likely to narrow in the future. An increasing proportion of the population will attend performing art events, which were earlier the province of a select few. The cost of attending special cultural occasions will fall due to an increasing integration of tourism and art consumption. There will also be some leeway to cater for special tastes, but it will become increasingly difficult to mount large original music festivals. However, it is to be expected that new, so far unknown, forms of art presentation will be invented.

The major factors curbing the rapid future growth of festivals are likely to come from the supply side. The advantage of comparatively low production costs is reduced by the larger number of festivals. They are no longer able to draw on the resources of the traditional venues at low or nominal costs because an increasing proportion of artistic performers have become freelance as a result of the great opportunities offered by festivals. As these special events become a regular feature, the supervisors of established opera houses, theatres, and concert halls will react and force the organizers of special cultural events to participate in the fixed costs. Many of the best-known and most prestigious festivals have become fully established: they often have buildings of their own and an increasing number of permanent staff. They share many features with conventional opera and concert houses: they have to cope with increasing government and trade union regulations and interference, and they rely ever more on a fixed set of visitors, with expectations shaped by the festival's traditions. As a result, many of the older festivals have become victims of their own success and find it difficult or impossible to engage in new artistic endeavours. Not surprisingly, some of these older festivals have given birth to new festivals trying to evade conventions and bureaucratic restrictions and break new artistic ground. Examples are the incontri musicali fuori programma, which have existed since 1978 at the Spoleto festival, or the various Fringes at the Edinburgh festival. However, it seems that even part of the Fringe in Edinburgh has already become established.

Even if the rapid rise in festivals cannot be expected to persist, they have had a strong and lasting impact on the art world. On the demand side, they have opened up art to an increasing proportion of the population. This popularization may not be in the interest of some art suppliers and art lovers, but it represents a considerable advance in catering for individual preferences. On the supply side, the increased competition between producers of art has transformed career patterns at theatres, opera houses, ballets, and orchestras and has led to a new relationship to both potential and actual art consumers. By subjecting art producers at least partly to the market, it has also favoured more efficient forms of organization and production in the world of art.

8.4 Conclusion

Classical music festivals are a welcome addition to the arts performed in fixed venues. They leave more room for artistic creativity, and they are able to cater for very specialized preferences, for instance for Baroque music played on contemporary instruments. Moreover, festivals are able to interest people who otherwise would never consider attending classical music performances in the performing arts. The danger is that festivals engage in excessive popularization and are too strongly influenced by business interests, such as commercial tourist organizations.

Related Literature

This chapter partly draws on

Frey BS, Vautravers-Busenhart I (2003) Special exhibitions and festivals: culture's booming path to glory. In: Frey BS (ed) Arts and economics. Springer, Heidelberg and New York, pp 67–94

Case studies of famous festivals are, for example

Frey BS (1986) The Salzburg festival: an economic point of view. J Cult Econ 10(2):27–44
Galeotti G (1992) Riflettori sull'iposcenio: elementi per un'analisi economica del festival di Spoleto. In: Brosio G, Santagata W (eds) Rapporto sull'economia delle arti e dello spettacolo in Italia. Fondazione Agnelli, Torino, pp 125–147

Chapter 9
Films

Abstract The success of a film is impossible to predict. A few of them are financially successful, while most of them are not. Actors are crucial to a film's success. As in other parts of the performing arts, a few superstars are greatly admired and highly compensated in a winner-take-all market while most of the other actors earn little. Consumers have many direct substitutes on which to spend their time and money: television, home video, DVD, internet, computer games, musical performances, and popular sport events such as football. Those with lower income and fewer time constraints tend to view mass films, while high-quality movies are mostly viewed by well-educated young city-dwellers.

Keywords Superstars · Winner-take-all market · Predictability · Financial success · Flops · Substitutes · Most successful films · American best films · Revenue · European critics · Actors · Film festivals · Movie awards

9.1 Characteristics

A salient feature of films is that their success is largely unpredictable. Even producers with extensive experience undertake movie projects that turn out to be financial flops. Even sophisticated techniques for predicting future demand rarely work. A partial exception is that of sequels of highly successful films, for instance *The Terminator*, directed by James Cameron with Arnold Schwarzenegger in the leading role. It was produced as a B-movie but became one of the most successful science fiction pictures. Four sequels followed in 1991, 2003, 2009, and 2015, and more are planned. But this is a rare exception of the general rule.

The most successful films, the "blockbusters", are shown in Table 9.1. In most cases their success was a surprise.

The figures for gross revenue are only crude approximations, because it is never certain whether all gross incomes from all countries are included, nor whether part of the revenue includes indirect incomes.

The distribution of financial success of films is highly skewed. A few movies make very high net profits, while most films are not profitable compared to other

B. S. Frey, *Economics of Art and Culture*, SpringerBriefs in Economics,
https://doi.org/10.1007/978-3-030-15748-7_9

Table 9.1 The ten financially most successful films

Title	Year	Worldwide gross revenue (in $ billion, constant $)
Gone with the Wind	1939	$ 3.6
Avatar	2009	$ 3.2
Titanic	1997	$ 3.0
Star Wars	1965	$ 3.0
The Sound of Music	2015	$ 2.5
E.T., the Extra-Terrestrial	1982	$ 2.4
The Ten Commandments	1956	$ 2.3
Doctor Zhivago	1965	$ 2.2
Jaws	1975	$ 2.1
Star Wars: The Force Awakens	2015	$ 2.1

(*Source* Guinness World Records; inflation adjustment by the consumer price index of IMF)

Table 9.2 American best films

Citizen Kane	1941
Casablanca	1943
The Treasure of Sierra Madre	1948
12 Angry Men	1957
Psycho	1960
The Godfather	1972

investments or even make a loss. Extreme events dominate; revenues decline strongly when a film proves to be unpopular with the potential audience.

Blockbusters can hardly be considered of high artistic value. Lists of the "best films of all time" feature quite different movies. The criteria used to decide what is the "highest quality" differ widely. Therefore, many different rankings exist. There is some agreement among critics that the following films count among the best (Table 9.2).

This list only considers American pictures. European critics are likely to also name the following films (see Table 9.3).

Of course, many high-quality films are produced in yet other countries. It suffices to name a few striking examples (see Table 9.4).

Or the highly praised pictures by Ingmar Bergman, for example (see Table 9.5).

Another feature of movies is the critical influence of actors. As in other parts of the performing arts, a few are superstars in a winner-take-all market who are greatly admired and receive huge compensation while most of the other actors earn little. Such movie superstar actors are, for example (see Table 9.6).

Whether these superstars are also the best actors is open to debate.

Table 9.3 Best films judged by European critics

Germany	The Cabinet of Dr. Caligari	1920
	Metropolis	1927
	Der blaue Engel	1930
	M – Eine Stadt sucht einen Mörder	1931
	Aguirre, der Zorn Gottes	1972
France	La Grande Illusion	1937
	Hiroshima Mon Amour	1959
	Hors du Souffle	1960
	Belle du Jour	1967
	Le Charme discret de la Bourgoisie	1972
Italy	Roma, Città aperta	1945
	Ladri di Biciclette	1948
	Notte di Cabiria	1956
	La Dolce Vita	1960

Table 9.4 Other high-quality films

Soviet Union	Battleship Potemkin	1925
Japan	Rashamon	1950

Table 9.5 Films by Ingmar Bergman

Sweden	Sommarlek (Summer Interlude)	1951
	Det sjunde inseglet (The Seventh Seal)	1957
	Tystnaden (Silence)	1963
	Scener ur et äktenskap (Scenes from a Marriage)	1973

9.1.1 Supply Side

The production of films is sequential and is composed of development, actual recording, and distribution. At each stage, teams are formed from a large pool of directors, artists, technicians, and administrators, a task requiring considerable coordination. Once a film has been recorded, the costs are sunk and cannot be recovered. Often, projected costs are hugely overrun. The movie *Titanic* was budgeted at $ 100 million, but ended up costing $ 200 million.

Three types of prices are set: the admission price in the cinema, the rental price for the film, and the distribution fee for marketing, advertising, and release on TV, video, and the internet. Many of these activities are characterized by increasing returns to scale. Average costs fall the more a film appeals to the public. As a consequence, the profits between films are highly skewed. Producers try to adjust these prices to the success of the movie. Cinemas have to pay a higher rental price for a very popular film.

Table 9.6 Movie superstars

Hollywood: actors	Tom Cruise
	Tom Hanks
	Harrison Ford
	Jonny Depp
	Jack Nicholson
	Leonardo DiCaprio
Hollywood: actresses	Cameron Diaz
	Emma Stone
	Sandra Bullock
	Jennifer Aniston
	Julia Roberts
France: actors	Alain Delon
	Gérard Depardieu
	Michel Piccoli
France: actresses	Jeanne Moreau
	Catherine Deneuve
	Brigitte Bardot
Germany: actors	Heinz Rühmann
	Curd Jürgens
	Mario Adorf
Germany: actresses	Hildegard Knef
	Lilli Palmer
	Romy Schneider
Switzerland: actors	Bruno Ganz
	Maximilian Schell
Switzerland: actresses	Liselotte Pulver
	Maria Schell

Movies are produced in many countries of the world. The Indian film industry, Bollywood, is the biggest producer, followed by Hollywood. Nigeria has a Nollywood. France, Germany, Spain, the United Kingdom, and Brazil also produce a considerable number of films. The national film industries are not monopolies but are concentrated in a few dominant studios. As the cost disease also applies to film production to some extent, in most countries the industry is subsidized by the government as a defence against dominance by Hollywood as well as to promote national culture. This government intervention can lead to a tension between financial success and artistic quality. Often, subsidies go to films that have high artistic goals but attract a small audience. All too often, neither high quality nor high box-office returns are reached.

Table 9.7 Famous art film festivals

Location	Foundation	Main Award
Venice	1932	Leone d'Oro
Cannes	1946	Palme d'Or
Berlin	1951	Goldener Bär
Locarno	1946	Pardo d'Oro
Karlovy Vary	1946	Crystal Globe
Toronto	1976	People's Choice Award
Tokyo	1985	Tokyo Grand Prix
Shanghai	1993	Golden Goblet Award

Film festivals are prominent in propagating this kind of art. Table 9.7 lists some prominent film festivals, their date of foundation and the major awards bequeathed.

The "Big Three" film festivals are Venice, Cannes, and Berlin. Many such festivals bequeath much-coveted awards, for instance in the case of the Berlin International Film Festival "Golden Bears", in Locarno "Leopards", in Cannes the "Palme d'Or" and in Toronto the "People's Choice Award". Receiving such prizes strongly boosts the recognition of the films, the directors, actors, and actresses.

9.1.2 Demand Side

Consumers have a choice of many direct substitutes to the cinema: television, home video, DVD, internet, computer games, musical performances, and popular sport events such as football. Viewing a film in a cinema requires considerable time, at least 90 min, and is close to the time required to attend theatrical, operatic, and orchestral performances. In addition, there are time costs for reaching the cinema, which are higher for individuals who have other attractive opportunities, be these earning money or spending their leisure time otherwise. Overwhelmingly, those with lower income and fewer time constraints attend mass films. This is different for high-quality movies that generally make greater cognitive demands of their audiences and are shown in specialized art cinemas. These films are mostly viewed by young, well-educated, liberal city-dwellers.

Film lovers today have many opportunities to watch movies outside the cinema through online rentals or other offers on the internet. While movies are protected by copyright laws, a great deal of unauthorized copying occurs. Such activities are a major handicap for film producers, as they forgo part of the possible revenue. In the future, new forms of contracts must be devised to allow film producers to reap a larger part of the benefits accruing to consumers.

9.2 Conclusion

The movie industry is faced with huge uncertainty. It is virtually impossible to predict which films will draw large audiences. The production of films is subject to strongly increasing returns to scale. Accordingly, most suppliers seek to produce popular films without much artistic quality. The government steps into support film projects that promise high quality. All too often, these productions only find a small audience and disappear quickly from the scene, leaving no lasting artistic or commercial impact.

Related Literature

Many important aspects of the movie industry are well analysed in

Simonton DK (2011) Great flicks. Scientific studies of cinematic creativity and aesthetics. Oxford University Press, Oxford, New York

A broad picture of the broadcasting and media industry is provided in

Caves R (2005) Switching channels: organization and change in TV broadcasting. Harvard University Press, Cambridge, MA, USA
Doyle G (2013) Understanding media economics. Sage, London
Vogel HL (2010) Entertainment industry economics: a guide for financial analysis, 8th edn. Cambridge University Press, London

Chapter 10
Museums

Abstract Major determinants of museum visits are entry fee, visitors' income and education, the quality of the collection, the attractiveness of the building, and the levels of amenities and marketing activities. Museums produce social non-use values: options, existence, bequest, prestige, and education, for which they are not compensated in monetary terms. Impact studies tend to focus on purely material effects of museums which is most questionable. The supply of museums is characterized by high fixed costs for buildings, collections, and staff. Blockbuster exhibitions, differentiating entry fees, and enlarging commercial activities can also raise revenue. The behaviour of purely public and private museums differs substantially. In both organizations, the directors are reluctant to sell any part of their holdings, even when under financial stress.

Keywords Entrance fee · Pricing options · Income · Education · Collection · Storage · Monetization · Buildings · Architecture · Amenities · Marketing · Blockbuster exhibitions · Commercial activities · Public museums · Private museums · Social demand · Revealed behaviour · Compensating variation · Popular referenda · Impact studies · Donations · Museum directors · Institutional conditions

10.1 Types of Museums

Museums play a substantial role in people's leisure activities. They belong to one of the most important tourist attractions.

There are several types of museums. It is useful to distinguish:

- *Content*. Most importantly art, historical artefacts, scientific objects, and many other exhibits of general and sometimes very specific interest;
- *Size*. Some museums occupy a large space, employ a high number of staff and have many thousands of visitors per day. Many others are of only local interest, are small, with very restricted opening hours, are run by amateur staff, and have few visitors;

B. S. Frey, *Economics of Art and Culture*, SpringerBriefs in Economics,
https://doi.org/10.1007/978-3-030-15748-7_10

- *Age*. Some museums have a long and distinguished history, while others are newly founded;
- *Institutional form*. Traditionally, European museums have been public, even forming part of the normal government administration. But there have always been private museums. Most museums lie somewhere between public and private.

10.2 Demand for Museums

10.2.1 Private Demand by Visitors

Museum visitors may be interested in the exhibits as a leisure activity or as part of their profession as art dealers or art historians. Visits may be undertaken by individuals and families and may be part of an organized activity involving, for instance, schools and firms.

There are three major determinants relating to prices and costs:

- *Entrance fee*. Together with the number of visits, this determines the revenue gained. The price elasticity indicates the percentage decrease in the number of visitors when the entrance fee is raised by a given percentage. Econometric estimates for a large number of diverse museums in different countries suggest that the demand for museum services is price inelastic. Zoos, science museums, and natural history museums show the largest price sensitivity, probably due to stronger competition from other leisure pursuits. Overall, the low price elasticities suggest that museums can generate significant increases in revenues through increasing admission fees.
- *Opportunity cost of time*. This indicates what alternatives visitors have to forgo when they visit a museum. In order to measure the monetary value, one must identify how much additional income could have been gained during that period. For persons with high income and variable time use, mostly the self-employed, the opportunity cost of time is higher than for people of low income and fixed working hours. The latter are therefore expected to visit museums more often. The opportunity cost of a museum visit depends not only on the time actually spent in a museum, but also on how much time is required to get to the museum, and thus on location, parking facilities etc. The increased opportunity costs of time for wealthy people attending museums tend to offset the positive income effect. One has to separate the two effects to find a positive income and a negative opportunity cost effect on demand. For tourists, the opportunity costs of time tend to be lower than for local inhabitants, because they often visit a city with the purpose of visiting its museums.
- *Price of alternative activities*. These are, most importantly, substitute leisure activities, such as other cultural events (theatre, cinema), sports, dining out in restaurants, time spent with friends at home, etc. Even within the industry, museums may constitute a substitute for other museums. The higher the prices of such alter-

natives are, the higher museum attendance is. Complements also systematically influence the number of museum visits. Important costs are those incurred through travel, accommodation, and meals. The higher the costs are, the lower is the rate of museum visits. These complementary costs constitute a substantial share of the total cost.

Income is another classical determinant of the demand for museum visits. People with higher incomes can better afford to pay for museum visits. However, opportunity costs rise with income, as discussed before. Another important factor is the high correlation between income and education. Better-educated individuals have the human capital necessary to more fully enjoy museums than people with lower education. This factor plays a larger role in museums of modern art and history but a lesser one for museums of science and technology, especially for museums of transport (railways, cars, and space travel).

There are many additional determinants of museum visits. One is the quality of the collection or special exhibition. Others are the attractiveness of the building, the level of amenities provided by the museum, such as the general atmosphere, the extent of congestion in front of the exhibits, the cafés and restaurants, and the museum shop. Another important determinant is the marketing efforts made by a museum, especially through regular and attention-catching advertising. Taste is also an important determinant of the rate of museum visits. This is reflected in the fact that individuals who used to visit museums in the past are more likely to do so in the present and future.

10.2.2 Social Demand

Museums produce effects on people who do not actually visit them. These benefits cannot be captured by the museums as revenue.

Museums create social non-use values: options, existence, bequest, prestige, and education. The provision of these values is not compensated in monetary terms. As a consequence, museums have little interest in producing these values, and do so in a small extent, only.

Museums may also produce negative external effects whose costs are carried by other people. An example would be the congestion and noise that museum visitors inflict on a community.

The non-user benefits and costs have been empirically measured by using three techniques:

- *Representative surveys* of both visitors and non-visitors of a museum. The questionnaires have to be carefully designed in order to elicit the true willingness to pay for the various social values produced by a museum. In particular, the survey respondents have to be asked trade-off questions that make clear what other goods and services have to be given up in order to obtain these non-user effects.

- Another technique to capture the value of a museum relies on the *revealed behaviour* of individuals. One procedure is to estimate how much the property values increase in a city that has a museum. People are willing to pay more for a house or apartment in a city with a museum than an equivalent house or apartment in a location without such a museum. The same *compensating variation* can be computed by looking at wages. People are willing to work for lower compensation in a city that has a museum.
- A third technique to capture social values is to analyse the outcome of *popular referenda* on expenditures for museums. Switzerland's many referenda have been successfully used to identify the option, existence, and bequest values of buying two paintings by Picasso for the museum of art in Basel.

10.2.3 Effects on Markets

Museums produce monetary values for other economic actors. They create additional jobs and commercial revenue, particularly in the tourism and restaurant businesses. These expenditures create further expenditures (e.g. the restaurant owners spend more on food) and a multiplier effect results. Impact studies measuring the additional market effects are popular with politicians and administrators because such studies provide reasons to spend money on museums. However, these studies have to be interpreted with much care:

- Impact studies tend to focus on purely material issue. But the raison d'être of museums is to provide a certain type of cultural experience to its visitors as well as providing the non-user benefits discussed above.
- A museum's purpose is not to stimulate the economy; there are generally much better means to achieve that goal. For example, a theme park or an exhibition of racing cars may be much better at stimulating the economy. If one follows the line of argument of impact studies, one would have to give preference to whatever expenditure leads to greater economic stimulation.

10.3 Supply

10.3.1 Cost Structure

Museums are characterized by special conditions.

- *High fixed costs*. Museums in general operate with high fixed costs: buildings, collection, staff, insurance, technical outfits, and so forth cannot be varied in the short run. Independent of the output (e.g. numbers of visitors or numbers of exhibitions) the costs of running the museums remain essentially the same. The fixed costs, especially for the acquisition of paintings, increase when art market prices rise, and the insurance fees for paintings increase accordingly. Because variable costs constitute a relatively low fraction of the total costs, museums face decreasing unit costs.

- *Marginal costs are close to zero*. The marginal costs of a museum constitute crucial economic information for determining how much should be produced. They indicate how costs vary with output. The cost of an additional visitor is usually close to zero. If a museum sets up an exhibition, the basic operating costs are for opening the museum on that particular day. When more people enter the museum, the fixed component can be divided by a larger quantity. Average costs therefore decrease. Were the number of visitors sufficient, such an industry could earn monopoly profits as it constitutes a natural monopoly. But this would be inefficient as the price—which reflects the marginal utility to consumers—is above the marginal cost. But demand is often insufficient; the demand curve lies below the average cost curve, and there is no price at which costs would be covered. However, there are situations in which marginal costs are not zero. At blockbuster exhibitions, an additional visitor does impose costs on other visitors. Such a congestion cost can be substantial.
- *Dynamic cost*. It is argued that museums face the same economic dilemma as most cultural organizations. Due to the cost disease, museums find it hard to raise the labour productivity of their employees but must follow the general wage increase that accompanies aggregate economic growth. Consequently, these organizations have constant financial problems. However, there are some possibilities for productivity advances in the museum industry: items can be shown on the internet; surveillance can be undertaken by cameras; organizational progress may rely on more volunteers; activities may be outsourced; and institutional settings may be changed, for instance by introducing New Public Management for public museums or privatizing them completely. All these changes work in the opposite direction of the cost disease.
- *High opportunity costs*. In their collected art works, museums own a huge endowment of high value. The paintings produce both storage and conservation costs and opportunity costs. The real costs of this capital stock would become apparent if museums borrowed money to buy the works of art. The annual interest that the museum would have to pay constitutes the real costs of capital. The opportunity cost of a painting is its monetary value used in an alternative investment. The annual rate on return can thus be seen as the cost of the artwork. For most museums, the value of their holdings is by far their greatest asset. At least some museums have realized that a closed museum costs more than just the operating expenses of the building. There are alternative uses for the rooms of the museum. The museum can, for instance, rent out rooms for business lunches and social events.

Most museums do not put a value on their collection in their accounts. Museums understate their true capital costs by not taking opportunity costs into account. This practice leads to an understatement of the losses and an overstatement of potential revenues. A productive unit should choose its outcome level by comparing costs and revenue. If all costs are not taken into account, museums attain too large a size.

10.3.2 Firm Structure

Museums can take various organizational forms. Mainly, they can be private for-profit organizations, private non-profit organizations, and public organizations run in a non-profitable way. For Europe and for the United States, the non-profit organizational form is the predominant structure for museums. Different hypotheses can be advanced to explain the dominance of non-profit firms in the museum world and the arts in general. Non-profit organizations were founded to help meet an unsatisfied demand for public goods. Alternatively, the cost structure of museums can explain part of the predominance of non-profit organizations.

Most museums face a demand curve that lies below the average cost curve. This makes it impossible to set a price at which total admission receipts cover the total cost of the museum. If price discrimination is not applicable, or only of limited use, arts organizations can still ask individuals for voluntary price discrimination. Visitors volunteer to pay more than the official admission price and thus become donors. The non-profit form is better than the for-profit enterprise in attracting donations, because consumers lack exact information about the quality of the goods and services provided. Donors then prefer non-profit firms, where the possibility that the managers of the firm exploit donors and consumers is taken to be more limited.

10.4 Museum Behaviour

The output a museum produces is not given but can be chosen by the art organization—as can the input and the technology used. As resources are scarce, museums have to make decisions where the emphasis should be. Should they produce a lot of exhibitions, and so increase the number of visitors, or should they put more emphasis on raising additional income in restaurants and shops?

Instead of taking for granted that managers of museums behave entirely in the interests of the museums, imagine that the directorate is concerned primarily with the personal utility of its members. The directors' utility depends on their own incomes and the prestige they obtain within their reference group, which consists mainly of art lovers and the international museum community. A second source of amenity is derived from the agreeable working conditions and job security. But the museum directorate is not free to simply pursue its own goals, because its members face certain constraints on their actions. Differences in these institutionally determined restrictions explain the museum management's behaviour.

The finances available are the most important constraint on the museum's directorate. Other constraints, such as limited space and legal and administrative burdens imposed by bureaucracy and labour unions can also weigh heavily. The source of income differs considerably between museums. While some depend mostly on public grants, others rely exclusively on private money, such as donations, sponsorship, and income generated from entrance fees, shops, and restaurants.

Purely public museums. Directors of purely public museums rely mostly on public grants. The government allocates them funds to cover the expenses considered necessary for fulfilling their tasks. While they are expected to keep within the budget, if a deficit occurs, it will be covered by the public purse. This institutional setting provides little incentive to generate additional income and to keep costs within budget. The directorate will not allocate energy and resources generating additional income, because any additional money goes back into the national treasury. If they were to make a surplus, the public grants would correspondingly decrease, which acts as an implicit tax of 100% on profits. The museum's management tends to emphasize non-commercial aspects. When the directorate is not forced to cover costs using its own efforts, it can legitimize its activities by referring to intrinsic artistic, scientific, and historical values. This application of non-commercial standards helps the museum directors to achieve their goal of prestige, top performance, and pleasant working conditions. These conditions lead to the following behaviour:

- Public museums do not sell any work of art from their art collection because the directorate cannot use the income generated. Moreover, selling works of art may attract criticism from politicians, especially if their value afterwards rises above the selling price.
- Directors of public museums are little interested in the number of visitors as such, but they depend on it in the longer run. In the budgetary process by the public administration their activity is often evaluated simply in terms of the number of visitors—not their contribution to what can be considered the public good. Therefore, exhibitions tend to be designed to please an insider group of art adepts.
- As a consequence, at least in the past visitors' amenities in public museums often were poorly developed. Relatively little attention was paid to the profitability of museum shops, restaurants, and cafeterias.

Purely private museums. Directors of purely private museums, on the other hand, have a strong incentive to increase their income, because their survival depends on money from entrance fees, the restaurant, shop, and additional money from sponsors and donors. If private museums generate a surplus, they are able to use it for future undertakings. As a result,

- Private museums rely on the market when managing their collection. Museums actively sell paintings that no longer fit the collection and use the money to buy new works of art.
- Private museums are more concerned with attracting visitors. Blockbuster exhibitions guarantee that the museum will earn revenue, because the preferences of a larger group of people are taken into account. Hence, the exhibitions are better arranged from a didactic point of view, appealingly presented, and above all the works of art are shown in a context attractive to a large crowd.

- Private museums emphasize visitors' amenities. The museum directorate makes an effort to satisfy the preferences of the visitors.

The difference in behaviour between public and private museums has narrowed over the last decades. Both public and private museums seek to attract funds from outside in order to be able to mount large special exhibitions and to cover their deficits. In contrast, if museums gain substantial revenues from the museum shop and restaurant, support from both the government and private sponsors tends to be reduced.

The performance of both types of museums tends to be evaluated by the number of visitors. In earlier times, this was not the case; museums were considered to be socially valuable by their mere existence. Today, all types of museums make a great effort to attract as many visitors as possible. These activities sometimes go so far that public museums almost behave like private museums. This raises the question why there are public museums at all.

Museums dependent on donations. Contributions to non-profit museums may be deductible under the income tax rule for individuals and corporations in certain countries. When the marginal tax rate falls, donations become less attractive. Tax-deductible status affects behaviour fundamentally. There is every incentive to avoid profits by charging low prices (which strengthens the legitimacy of tax-deductible status), while there is also an incentive to take out profits in the form of various kinds of excess payments that show up as costs.

Museum directors have a strong incentive to attract donors. They devote a great deal of effort and skilled resources to this end. Donors can be pleased in various ways, which influences the behaviour of the museum management. Donors can exercise some measure of control over the activities of museums. They directly influence museum policy by either interfering in the programming or by setting strongly binding legal limitations on the collections they donate. Most donors want to highlight their own artistic visions. Museums dependent on donations are rarely able to manage their collections on the market, which imposes considerable opportunity costs on museums.

A donor can be pleased when a museum publicizes the donor's contribution, thus enhancing their prestige and social status. Museums have developed an elaborate system of honours ranging from appropriate attributes ("benefactor", "patron", "contributor", etc.), to naming rooms, wings, and even whole buildings after the donor.

Museums must give the impression that the donations are effectively used. The art institution's good reputation with the public and the media is crucial for the flow of donations. This induces the museum directorate to use the museum's money efficiently.

10.5 Collection Management

In most art museums in the world, a considerable proportion of the holdings of paintings (often 80 to 90%) is not exhibited and not accessible, except possibly to specialists. The holdings then serve a solely archival role. What constitutes the major part of the wealth of an art museum does not appear in the balance sheet; the bookkeeping procedure of art museums does not even mention that the paintings collected are of any value, although at today's art market prices, collections of even minor museums are likely to be worth dozens of millions of Euro. In the case of major museums, the value may amount to many hundreds of millions of Euro. The museum managers are well aware that their holdings are very valuable. But why do managers systematically disregard these large sums of money? Three reasons can be proposed to explain the behaviour of museum management:

- One reason may be that the government imposes a legal constraint on selling. Many, or even most, public museums in continental Europe are prohibited from selling their art work. It is often allowed in the United States and to a lesser extent also in Britain.
- There may be voluntary contracts between the museum directorate and donors, who often want to keep the collection they give intact and often require it to be shown in particular rooms. The directorate is faced with a trade-off between receiving additional paintings and having to accept additional restrictions. If it decides to accept the gift, its value must be higher than the cost of the restrictions involved. Today, few museums accept such restrictions attached to a donation.
- The most convincing explanation for the behaviour is the effect of institutional conditions. For public museums, the museum directorate has no incentive to sell its holdings in storage. When a painting is sold, the revenue gained is not added to the museum's disposable income but, according to the rules of the public administration in most countries, goes into the general public treasury. Even if this is not the case, the budget allocated to the museum is most likely to be correspondingly reduced. This institutional setting dampens all incentives to manage the collection on the market. Selling paintings means that the existing stock of art is at least partly monetized, which eases outside interference by politicians and parliamentarians with the museum's business. The museum directorate's performance becomes easier to evaluate, and the buying and selling prices of particular paintings can be compared. As long as the criteria for evaluation are exclusively of an art-historical nature, the museum community is to a substantial extent able to define its performance itself. This is a useful and successful survival strategy that museum administrations do not voluntarily relinquish.

  In contrast, private American art museums are indeed active in selling and buying art in order to suit their purposes.

Collections serve an important function by mounting special exhibitions. An art museum can only borrow paintings from another museum if it is able to reciprocate in the future. This establishes a club-like situation in which only museums with valuable holdings are able to participate.

10.6 Entrance Fees

There are large differences between museums in the way they set their entrance fees. Mr Sloane, whose donation led to the founding of the British Museum, imposed an explicit restriction not to charge an entrance fee. Still today, most British museums do not charge their visitors. Even in the United States, some museums, in particular the national ones, do not levy an explicit entrance fee. There are some positive externalities connected with a museum, as discussed before. Therefore, the museum should be funded with tax money. But the benefits are not distributed equally, and an accurate taxation according to these benefits is almost impossible. Those who visit a museum probably benefit the most from the museum. Therefore, an entrance fee should be levied over and above the contribution from general taxation. In the system of free admission, all taxpayers have to carry the total cost of running a museum, but the lower income groups who rarely visit museums are also burdened by the necessary taxation.

A variety of pricing options exists besides free entrance: donation boxes with and without price suggestions, seasonal tickets with zero marginal pricing for a particular entry, a free day policy, and a more sophisticated price discrimination. Price discrimination can be undertaken at times of high demand and/or with respect to the type of visitor. Many museums, even those that do not charge for their permanent collection, have higher entrance fees for special exhibitions. Additionally, a museum can charge more at weekends and less during summer holidays. Tourists could be charged more than residents. Prices can also be differentiated between visitors who want to spend little time on the visit to a museum and those who want to spend ample time. In periods of high demand, when the art museum's capacity is fully used, two entry fees can be set, a high and a low one. The high-priced entry will have a correspondingly shorter queue and will be used by the first category of visitors. The low-priced entry option will be used by the second category of visitors, among them students and other young people who do not want to spend much money but have plenty of time at their disposal. Price differentiation is advantageous for both categories of visitors (one gets in more quickly, the other pays less) and for the museum administration, which can therefore raise its revenue.

The question of how pricing influences the finances of the museum not only depends on the price elasticity of demand. Charging can also influence the flow of public subsidies and donations. Moreover, pricing decisions can influence the income generated with ancillary goods; for instance, revenue from the shop and restaurant depends on the number of visitors.

10.7 Commercial Activities

Besides the core activities of museums, which are directly related to the works exhibited or stored, most museums also engage in ancillary activities. The revenues from these activities can make a large contribution to cover operating costs. Museums operate museum shops, restaurants, and cafés, sell catalogues, make money from parking lots, and organize cultural trips. Today, several museums not only operate shops on the museum's premises but even run off-site stores in the city the museum is located in, or even in a totally different city.

10.8 Conclusion

Due to the cost disease and the free provision of social non-use values, many museums are in constant financial distress. There are several possibilities to mitigate this problem. A museum can gain additional revenue by organizing blockbuster exhibitions. However, the costs of doing so are substantial, in particular due to high insurance and transport costs. A museum can also gain additional revenue by charging higher prices for visitors with low price elasticity, and it can engage in more commercial activities such as running profitable museum shops and renting out the museum space for social occasions. The policy of not selling any part of the collection needs to be reconsidered. There should be more flexibility in this regard. For instance, works never shown to the public could be sold to another institution prepared to exhibit them.

Related Literature

This chapter uses parts of the following joint paper

Frey BS, Meier S (2006) The economics of museums. In: Ginsburgh VA, Throsby D (eds) Handbook of the economics of art and culture. Elsevier, Amsterdam, pp 1018–1047

A fundamental contribution to the topic is

Hansmann HB (1981) Nonprofit enterprise in the performing arts. Bell J Econ 12(2):341–361

Excellent discussions of art museums, especially for the case of the United States, are provided by

DiMaggio PJ (ed) (1986) Nonprofit enterprise in the arts. Studies in mission and constraint, Oxford University Press, New York, Oxford
Feldstein M (ed) (1991) The economics of art museums. Chicago University Press, Chicago

More general aspects are the subject of

Weisbrod BA (ed) (1998) To profit or not to profit: the commercial transformation of the nonprofit sector. Cambridge University Press, Cambridge, UK

Chapter 11
Superstar Museums and Special Exhibitions

Abstract Superstar museums are a "must-see" for tourists and have achieved cult status. They attract large and increasing numbers of visitors and have a major impact on the local economy. Superstar museums feature paintings by world-famous painters and prominent architectural design. Their income stems to a significant extent from the revenue of the museum bookshops and restaurants. Most art museums run a special exhibition of some sort. They attract new groups of visitors, focus attention on the museum and on the exhibits, and enable lucrative sponsoring revenue to be gained. The cost of mounting such exhibitions is relatively low. They allow more artistic creativity than is possible with the museums' own collection.

Keywords Most visited art museums · Must-see · Cult status · World famous-painters · Blockbuster exhibitions · Architecture · New visitor groups · Attention · Media · Exhibits · Sponsoring · Commercialization · Total experience · Amenities · Production cost · Creativity

11.1 Characteristics of Superstar Museums

There are a few well-known and world-famous museums. They can be called superstar museums because they have a special status setting them far apart from other museums. Table 11.1 gives a selection of some of the best-known art museums in the world.

Superstar museums have five notable features:

- Superstar museums are a "must-see" for tourists. Such museums are featured prominently in guidebooks. Superstar museums have achieved a cult status that almost everyone is aware of. Few tourists visit for example, one of the cities listed in Table 11.1 without visiting its superstar museum.
- Superstar museums have large numbers of visitors and have experienced a dramatic increase in the numbers of visitors. As Table 11.1 shows, superstar museums have visitor numbers ranging from more than 1 million to the Art Institute of Chicago and to the Kunsthistorisches Museum in Vienna to more than 8 million to the Louvre in Paris.

B. S. Frey, *Economics of Art and Culture*, SpringerBriefs in Economics,
https://doi.org/10.1007/978-3-030-15748-7_11

Table 11.1 A selection of superstar museums of art

Museum	Location	Number of visitors per year (2017, in millions)
Louvre	Paris	8.1
Metropolitan Museum of Art	New York	6.7
Vatican Museums	Rome	6.4
Tate Modern	London	5.7
National Gallery of Art	Washington	5.2
National Gallery	London	5.2
State Hermitage	Saint Petersburg	4.2
Reina Sofia	Madrid	3.9
Prado	Madrid	2.8
Museum of Modern Art	New York	2.8
Rijksmuseum	Amsterdam	2.2
Galleria degli Uffizi	Florence	2.2
Art Institute of Chicago	Chicago	1.6
Kunsthistorisches Museum	Vienna	1.4

– Superstar museums feature world-famous paintings by world-famous painters. The collections in large museums comprise works by thousands of artists; only a few of them are known to art lovers, let alone to the average visitor. Museums wanting to attract a large crowd concentrate on a few superstar artists. Some paintings are known to virtually everyone in the Western world and far beyond. Examples include the *Nightwatch* in Amsterdam's Rijksmuseum and *Las Meninas* in the Prado. The quintessential superstar painting is Leonardo's *Mona Lisa*. The Louvre has responded by indicating a direct route to the *Mona Lisa* right at the entrance. Even the Vatican Museum now posts the (more or less) direct route to another world-famous work of art, Michelangelo's frescos in the Sistine Chapel. From the visitors' point of view, even very large museums are closely associated with or defined by very few, often one or two, paintings: the superstar phenomenon. Museums are not only the proud owners of these masterpieces; they are also their captives. They are forced to exhibit them, but this also means that their other paintings lose prominence.
– Superstar museums often have an architectural design that makes the building itself a world-famous artistic feature. Examples include Frank Lloyd Wright's Guggenheim Museum in New York; Renzo Piano's Centre Pompidou in Paris; Mario Botta's San Francisco Museum of Modern Art; Frank Gehry's Guggenheim Museum in Bilbao, Richard Meier's Getty Center in Los Angeles; and Jacques Herzog and Pierre de Meuron's Tate Modern in London.
– Superstar museums are commercialized in two respects: A significant part of their income derives from the revenue of the museum bookshops and museum restaurants. And superstar museums have a major impact on the local economy.

Superstar museums differ in the importance of these five characteristics. Ideally, they must fully meet all of them; the Musée du Louvre is an example, the architectural feature being Ming Pei's pyramid at the entrance. Other superstar museums are very strong in some characteristics, while barely meeting others. An example of this phenomenon is the Getty Museum in Los Angeles, which excels in its architecture, including its location, but does not have as many paintings by world-famous artists as other superstar museums.

Although some art museums have reached the status of superstars and become household names to hundreds of millions of people, only a few museums attain this rank. Those that do are mostly associated with major tourist cities, which in turn owe part of their prominence to the superstar museums. One may even argue that there are "super-super-star" museums—the Louvre, the Metropolitan and the Vatican. They have such famous and extensive holdings that one would think that they do not even have to mount special exhibitions; they nevertheless attract a huge number of visitors.

Superstar museums are able to exploit the economies of scale by being known to a large number of people. These museums are not only featured in newspapers and on the radio and TV but can raise enough money to produce their own videos and virtual museums. These costs are essentially independent of the number of consumers and therefore favour the major museums, because the set-up costs are normally too large for smaller institutions. While the latter will certainly catch up (a homepage is a matter of course for all museums), the major museums will have the funds to improve their scope and quality so as to maintain their lead. Superstar museums have started to establish museum networks. Thus, for example, the London Tate Gallery has spawned satellite museums at Liverpool and St. Ives, and the Prado has started to lend out about one third of its holdings to museums in the provinces.

Superstar museums find themselves in a new competitive situation. Their frames of reference shift from other museums in the city or region to other superstar museums. This competition between the superstars extends over a broad area, including commercial activities and sponsors.

The superstar museums must make a huge effort to stay in that category. Frantic activities are therefore often undertaken: special exhibitions are organized in the hope that they turn out to be blockbusters, visitors' amenities are improved (e.g. a larger variety of fancy restaurants), and new buildings with stunning architectural designs are added (e.g. in the case of New York's Museum of Modern Art). The superstar status tends to transform museums into providers of "total experience". This new role stands in stark contrast to the traditional notion of museums as preservers of the past.

The total experience offered by the superstar museums, and demanded by the huge crowds of visitors, must meet two conditions:

- Art must be placed in the context of history, technology, and well-known events in politics and entertainment, such as motion pictures. Superstar museums are forced constantly to also embed the permanent collection in a context attractive to large numbers of visitors.

– Superstar museums must be able to provide a wide range of amenities, not unlike entertainment parks. The activities offered extend beyond cafés, restaurants, and museum shops. The Louvre, for example, opened a large underground shopping mall called "Le Carrousel du Louvre". Activities of superstar museums comprise all sorts of educational activities, not only for children but also for adults, and most importantly, plain entertainment.

11.2 Special Exhibitions

There is hardly an art museum not running, or at least preparing, a special exhibition of some sort. Such an exhibition may feature one particular artist, often in commemoration of his or her birth or death, or a group of artists; may focus on a period or a genre of paintings; or may establish a connection to some historical event.

Table 11.2 shows some of the most successful blockbuster exhibitions.

Some special exhibitions are composed solely of paintings from the holdings of the organizing museum, but most such special shows bring together works of art from various museums and private collections. Once collated, large temporary exhibitions frequently travel to other museums cooperating with the organizer. Some exhibitions, indeed, are designed from the beginning to be sent to various countries. Quite often, important museums simultaneously display several shows, which they have either mounted themselves or received from other organizers.

Museum exhibitions do not always meet with enthusiasm. The director of the Metropolitan Museum of Art, Philippe de Montebello, complained that whenever he meets people, they ask him what show he is presently preparing, to which he retorts that he is the director of the Metropolitan Art Museum and not the Metropolitan Opera.

Special exhibitions and festivals are closely related in various important respects.

Table 11.2 Blockbuster exhibitions, 1963–2014

Content	Year	Museum
Mona Lisa	1963	Metropolitan Museum of Art, New York
The Treasure of Tutankhamun	1976–77	National Gallery of Art, Washington DC
Turner	1983–84	Grand Palais, Paris
Cézanne	1996	Philadelphia Museum of Art
China's Terracotta Army	2007–08	British Museum London
Ashura and Masterpieces from Kohfukuji	2009	Tokyo National Museum
Master of Impressionism—Claude Monet	2014	Art Mall, Shanghai

11.2.1 Demand Side

- *High Income Effect*. Consumers tend to spend an increasing proportion of their rising incomes on visiting art exhibitions.
- *Attracting New Groups of Visitors*. Many people are overawed by the "temples of culture", feel insecure and unwelcome, and therefore do not even consider visiting the local art museum. This is less the case for special exhibitions, which are broadly advertised and which are made attractive to new groups. This is partly overcome by "dressing up the museum": special exhibitions are always marked by huge banners and other advertising ploys and even the museum entrances are made welcoming. Extensive promotion also plays a role.
- *Focusing Attention*. An exhibition seeks to attract consumers by presenting some extraordinary and special cultural experience. As a result, visitors interested in a particular form of art come together, often from distant locations. This development is, of course, supported by low and falling travel costs. Public attention is drawn away from the permanent collection towards a special and unique (or at least rare) event.
- *Newsworthiness*. Special exhibitions are news and thus attract the attention of television, radio, and the print media, which is otherwise impossible to obtain to the same degree, especially free of charge. Such exhibitions are also featured in the social media. It is easy to persuade media people to report on a special exhibition, while the permanent collection hardly ever makes any news.
- *Location and Timing*. Special exhibitions are mostly organized by major museums, which are located in large cities, so the period outside summer holidays is more attractive. Winter is a good season for special art exhibitions as prospective visitors are prepared to travel to these centres, thus combining holidays with a cultural experience.
- *Low price elasticity*. Managers of special exhibitions have more leeway to increase their revenue by setting higher entrance fees. Entrance prices for special exhibitions are often much higher than for the permanent collection.

11.2.2 Supply Side

Several determinants of supply contrast with the conditions faced by the permanent venues and contribute to the success of special exhibitions.

- *Low Production Cost*. The absolute cost of special exhibitions is certainly high. The organizing museum has to cover the insurance and transport costs, which may be substantial. But it is low compared to the sum of money they would require if all the resource inputs used were attributed to these special events. Museum employees are taken to organize and run special exhibitions, but the corresponding cost is not attributed to the special events. One such cost is the neglect of cataloguing and maintaining the permanent collection. In addition, the museum rooms where the

special exhibitions are shown do not enter the costs as the forgone opportunities are not part of normal bookkeeping.
The costs of mounting a special exhibition are also significantly lowered because the art works shown do not have to be rented at market price. A rental market for art works only exists under very exceptional conditions and is of little importance. Rather, the exhibits are lent free of charge. The cost of such lending appears in a non-monetary form. The whole system of special exhibitions is built on mutual exchange or on the principle of reciprocity. Only museum directors who are prepared to lend art works from their own permanent collections are able to participate in this exchange system. The production costs can be further lessened by arranging travelling, circulating, or touring exhibitions, where costs can be shared by those museums showing the exhibition.

- *More creative possibilities*. Museum directors are bound by artistic conventions. The particular hanging of pictures at many museums has become part of cultural heritage, and it is next to impossible to rearrange the permanent collection to any significant extent. Special exhibitions offer a chance of avoiding such historical restrictions. One of the major tasks and potentials of an art exhibition is to arrange the art works so as to create new insights and effects. In addition, the assembly of art works from many different permanent collections provides a challenge to museum directors, curators, and exhibition and graphic designers to exert their artistic creativity and sense of innovation, and possibly to raise controversy—aspects which are highly valued by museum people, not only for their own sake, but also because it is beneficial for their careers.
- *Higher revenues*. Special exhibitions provide a good opportunity for directors of art museums to appropriate at least part of the extra revenue generated. Being an extraordinary event, the museum directors are in a good bargaining position vis-à-vis the public budgetary authorities to use some discretion where these funds are concerned and not be fully penalized by a reduction in future budget allocations.
- *Increased sponsoring*. Politicians and public officials have a pronounced interest in special grand exhibitions. Business sponsors want a well-defined, high-quality event aimed at a specific audience where they can present and advertise themselves.
- *Career opportunities*. Museum directors are increasingly chosen from, and transform themselves into, exhibition organizers, and move ever further away from being merely respected scientists and art experts. This change in the museums' career system may run into problems in the long run. There is a rising perception that travel of art works going with special exhibitions tends to reduce, and sometimes damage, the quality of art objects, which makes it increasingly difficult to collect the objects necessary to mount an attractive exhibition.

11.3 Conclusion

Superstar museums and blockbuster exhibitions are here to stay. They usefully attract people who otherwise do not visit museums, and they are able to attract attention to artists and artistic movements that are otherwise disregarded. They may also help to improve the financial situation of museums.

There are, however, major disadvantages. The normal collections of museums tend to be disregarded, and museums that do not have the capacity to engage in such activities become less important. Too much attention from the media, politicians, and the public goes to the few superstar museums and their special exhibitions.

Relevant Literature

This chapter is based on

Frey BS (2003) Superstar museums: an economic analysis. In: Arts and economics. Analysis and cultural policy, 2nd edn. Springer, Berlin, pp 49–65

The museums' handling of their collection is discussed in

Cantor JE (1991) The museum's collection. In: Feldstein M (ed) The economics of art museums. University of Chicago Press, Chicago, pp 17–23

Special exhibitions are the subject of

Belcher M (1991) Exhibitions in museums. Leicester University Press, Leicester

Chapter 12
Cultural Heritage

Abstract Cultural heritage is composed of built, moveable, intangible, and natural objects. Only a small proportion of their benefits are reflected in monetary form, but these are positive externalities. Not everything can be preserved, because this would block the further development of cities and regions. Many heritage goods have the property of a public good; people not paying a fee cannot be excluded from consumption. If the measured total benefits are superior to the total cost involved in keeping up a heritage object, a society is better off preserving it.

Keywords Built heritage · Moveable heritage · Intangible heritage · Natural heritage · Preservation · Public good · World Heritage Sites · Historical centres · Use values · Non-use values · Government intervention

12.1 Many Types of Cultural Heritage

The values that humanity has inherited from its ancestors take many different forms. They cannot usefully be defined; to some extent, their existence and value is socially constructed by the present generation. Four different types of cultural heritage may be distinguished:

- *Built Heritage*. This type comprises buildings, monuments, historic parts of human settlements, and other sites inherited from the past and considered to be worth preserving for future humanity due to their culture and symbolic value. Its preservation provides added utility to consumers compared to a state in which the components are dilapidated or disappear completely. In many cases, they have the characteristics of a public good and exhibit strong positive externalities. Their consumption is to a large extent non-rival; if one person admires an old square in a city, this does not interfere with other people also doing so. In most cases, consumers are not excludable, or there is no wish to exclude them.
  Built heritage is often publicly owned, for instance, important palaces and monuments.
- *Moveable Heritage*. This consists of artworks such as antiques, paintings, artefacts, and the content, of archives of old documents such as Holy Scriptures. This type

B. S. Frey, *Economics of Art and Culture*, SpringerBriefs in Economics,
https://doi.org/10.1007/978-3-030-15748-7_12

of cultural heritage is often privately owned by individuals, non-governmental organizations, or firms; an owner can to a considerable extent appropriate its value. Moveable heritage is easily saleable, including across countries and continents. Antiques, the objects found at ancient cultural sites, are often stolen and brought to national and international markets.

- *Intangible Heritage*. These are the works inherited from the past as literature and musical pieces, rituals, practices, skills, traditional knowledge, and languages. It includes the instruments, objects, and artefacts associated with these. As is the case for built heritage, intangible heritage has strong external effects and has the characteristics of a public good.
- *Natural Heritage*. They comprise national parks and other spectacular sites.

The United Nations, through its UNESCO organization, has compiled a list of 845 built heritage sites (as of July 2018) considered most important to preserve for humanity, as well as lists of moveable, intangible, and natural heritage. In addition, many lists compiled by national, regional, and local governments, non-governmental organizations, and clubs note the most important cultural heritage objects and traditions in particular regions or of particular types.

Table 12.1 provides a selection of some of the most famous built world heritage sites.

Table 12.1 only provides a small selection of the built heritage sites listed by UNESCO. They are not all ancient. For example, Sidney Opera House, designed by Jörn Utzen, and the Guggenheim Museum in Bilbao, built by Frank Gehry, are recent (1973 and 1997 respectively).

Table 12.2 gives some examples of well-known natural heritage cites.

UNESCO lists 209 natural heritage sites (as of July 2018); Table 12.2 only lists a small number of them.

Table 12.3 shows examples of intangible heritage items (only Europe).

This is again a small selection of 470 elements in 117 countries (as of July 2018). As can be seen, intangible heritage comprises extremely different cases.

12.2 Values Generated

Cultural heritage can be considered to be a capital stock subject to investment and depreciation and providing a rate of return to consumers in the benefits gained. Only a small proportion of this utility is reflected in monetary form. A large proportion is composed of positive externalities not captured by markets. There are two different types of value

- *Use values*. The benefits of an object of the cultural heritage is directly consumed by individuals, notably as tourists, and firms. A marginal evaluation reveals how much added value is gained by changes in an object's characteristics. This allows the benefits to be compared to an investment in other uses of the available resources.

Table 12.1 Selection of world heritage sites

Asia	Abu Simbel	Egypt
	The Pyramids	Egypt
	Taj Mahal	India
	The Forbidden City	China
	Ancient Kyoto	Japan
	Angkor Wat	Cambodia
	Petra	Jordan
	Bagan	Myanmar
South America	Machu Picchu	Peru
	Chichen Itza	Mexico
	Old Havana	Cuba
Australia	Sidney Opera House	Australia
North America	Statue of Liberty	United States of America
	City Center of Quebec	Canada
Europe	Acropolis Athens	Greece
	Stonehenge	England
	Tower of London, Westminster Palace and Westminster Abbey	England
	Mont Saint Michel	France
	Palace and Gardens of Versailles	France
	Cesky Krumlow	Czech Republic
	Venice	Italy
	Vatican City	Vatican/Italy
	Cologne Cathedral	Germany
	Guggenheim Museum Bilbao	Spain
Historical centres		
Europe	Rome, Florence, Pisa, Assisi, Verona	Italy
	Valetta	Malta
	Berne	Switzerland
	Edinburgh	Scotland
	Vienna, Salzburg	Austria
	Bruges	Belgium
	Sintra	Portugal
	Budapest	Hungary
	Krakow	Poland
	Tallinn	Estonia
	St. Petersburg	Russia

Table 12.2 Selection of natural heritage sites

Loire Valley	France
Easter Island	Chile
Galapagos Island	Ecuador
Great Barrier Reef	Australia
Iguazu National Park	Brazil and Argentina
Serengeti National Park	Tanzania
Grand Canyon	United States of America
Yellowstone National Park	United States of America

Table 12.3 Examples of intangible heritage items

Art of Neapolitan "Pizzaiuolo"	Italy
Basel Carnival	Switzerland
Beer culture	Belgium
Flamenco	Spain
Cante Alentejano	Portugal
French equestrian tradition	France
Ideas and practice of organizing shared interests in cooperatives	Germany

– *Non-use values*. These are the benefits derived from the existence of a heritage site; the option to visit it (even if one does not at the present time); the possibility of bequeathing it to descendants; the symbolic importance for society; the historic, aesthetic, and spiritual values pertaining to a heritage object; and the prestige going to the local, regional, and national communities. These are values not reflected in entry prices or other use values.

A direct method for capturing values not reflected by markets is to ask a representative sample of the population how much they are willing to pay to prevent the dilapidation of a built heritage or natural heritage site. Alternatively, they can be asked how much they are willing to pay to restore a building or a park to its former condition.

The value attributed to cultural heritage can also be captured by the revealed preferences of consumers. If they derive benefits from living, say, near a beautiful cathedral, they are willing to pay a higher rent for an apartment. The difference in the rent is an indication of the value attributed by these people to the cathedral. Another method considers the travel costs that people are willing to pay to visit, say, a famous cathedral. The corresponding sum is the lower bound of the utility created by the monument.

The various measurement methods are suited to capturing particular aspects of the utility created by a heritage site. For instance, a rent difference attributable to living close to a beautiful cathedral captures only the benefits generated for a small number of residents but not for other city-dwellers or tourists.

12.3 What and How to Preserve?

Objects of cultural heritage are confronted with the fundamental economic problem that not everything can be preserved. If this were the case, the further development of cities and regions would become impossible. There is a scarcity of options, and a reasoned choice is required. People acting in markets do not automatically compare the benefits and costs of each option. Rather, a large proportion of both the benefits and the costs are external to markets and must be captured by the methods described before. This holds even more strongly for heritage goods that have the property of a public good, meaning that those persons who do not pay a fee cannot be excluded from consumption. If the measured benefits are superior to the cost involved in preserving a heritage object, a society is better off preserving the site. Conversely, if other uses of resources, for instance demolishing an old building and erecting a new one, provides higher net benefits, the heritage site should not be preserved.

Such decisions are not easy to make. Most importantly, the measurement of non-use values is subject to considerable uncertainties. Another problem arises when a heritage object is owned by a private person or firm because the property rights in the object may be violated. An example is the owner of an old house, who has high costs in maintaining the building but could reap high monetary benefits by selling it to a developer. In such a situation, it is particularly important to evaluate the non-monetary benefits and costs of preserving the building carefully.

If it emerges that the total benefits of keeping an intact cultural building are superior to the total cost, it may be decided to preserve the building in its current condition, to restore it to its original condition, or to adapt it to a different use. Examples are churches that are no longer used for their religious function. They can be turned into bars, restaurants, or museums without destroying them, and keeping at least the external architecture intact.

The public sector may intervene directly by imposing regulations. In the case of buildings, this can involve restrictions on what may be altered, the specification of standards and materials used for restoration, or sale conditions, for instance preventing the sale of the property to a foreigner. These regulations may be legally binding or only advisory. In order to preserve a site, the government may rely on direct funding, subsidies, or tax expenditures through the provision of tax incentives.

Non-governmental institutions such as heritage organizations and private clubs may play a major role in the preservation of cultural heritage. They assist the public authorities, most importantly the administrators, in evaluating the value of cultural heritage. In addition, sponsorship by corporations seeking a good image in society, as well as individuals engaging in philanthropy, are important actors. Not least, people willing to volunteer, for instance by helping to supervise the visitors to famous churches, may play a significant role.

12.4 Conclusion

Heritage objects of all sorts are subject to large external effects or are public goods. The market for heritage sites does not lead to a socially beneficial degree of preservation. As the benefits tend to be reflected less by markets than the costs, there is a strong case for government intervention.

Decisions on what to preserve are difficult to take. The measurement of non-use values is subject to considerable uncertainties. Property rights in the object may be violated. It is therefore important to carefully evaluate the non-monetary benefits and costs of preserving the building. A major trade-off must be considered: saving our heritage versus allowing our society to develop further and to create new sites. If too much heritage is preserved, there is too little room for enterprising future design.

The public sector may intervene directly by imposing regulations or by buying the site. Non-governmental institutions, such as heritage organizations, private clubs, persons engaging in philanthropy, and corporations using sponsorship to seek a good image in society are important actors. In addition, people willing to volunteer should be involved.

Related Literature

Pathbreaking contributions are

Hutter M, Rizzo I (eds) (1997) Economic perspectives of cultural heritage. Palgrave Macmillan, London

Klamer A, Throsby D (2000) Paying for the past: the economics of cultural heritage. World Culture Report. UNESCO, New York, pp 130–145

Mossetto G, Vecco M (2001) Economia del patrimonio monumentale. F. Angeli, Venice

Peacock A (1998) Does the past have a future? The political economy of heritage. Institute of Economic Affairs, London

There are several very useful collections of articles that contain contributions to specific aspects of cultural heritage. For instance, the book edited by Rizzo and Mignosa contains case studies for various sites in the United Kingdom, China, Italy, Egypt, Japan, and Latin America

Rizzo I, Mignosa A (eds) (2013) Handbook on the economics of cultural heritage. Edward Elgar, Cheltenham

Rizzo I, Towse R (eds) (2002) The economics of heritage. Edward Elgar, Cheltenham

Chapter 13
UNESCO World Heritage List

Abstract The World Heritage List compiles built and natural sites and more recently also intangible traditions and customs judged to be of "outstanding value to humanity" by a commission of UNESCO. The main goals are to draw attention to sites and traditions in danger of disappearing and to assist in preserving them. There are some negative effects: questionable selection; undue political intervention; overextension; and attracting destruction in conflicts. There are alternatives to the UNESCO List. Sometimes no intervention is needed, in some cases market forces can be employed, and several other evaluations are available about what is worth preserving.

Keywords UNESCO · Selection · Attention · Protection · Political intervention · Overextension · Destruction · Alternatives to Heritage List · Competing evaluations · Random selection · Popular sites

13.1 Content of the List

The World Heritage List compiled by UNESCO has become highly popular. Many World Heritage Sites are major attractions for cultural tourism and icons of national identity.

In 1959, UNESCO launched a successful international campaign to save the Abu Simbel temples in the Nile Valley. The General Conference of UNESCO adopted the Convention Concerning the Protection of the World Cultural and Natural Heritage in November 1972. The Convention "seeks to encourage the identification, protection and preservation of cultural and natural heritage around the world considered to be of outstanding value to humanity". It came into force in 1977 and was ratified by 20 nations. The Convention now (July 2018) includes 193 countries and comprises 1,092 sites. The countries with most sites are Italy with 54, China 53, Spain 47, and France and Germany with 44 each.

The Convention's criterion of "outstanding value to humanity" is noble but has proven to be almost impossible to clearly define. Sites must fulfil three comprehensive criteria: uniqueness, historical authenticity, and integrity or intactness.

B. S. Frey, *Economics of Art and Culture*, SpringerBriefs in Economics,
https://doi.org/10.1007/978-3-030-15748-7_13

The World Heritage List is generally considered an excellent contribution to saving the globe's common history in the form of cultural monuments and landscapes.

13.2 Positive Aspects of the World Heritage List

The UNESCO List provides two beneficial consequences: the direction of attention and the specific protection provided.

13.2.1 Attention

The World Heritage List can be considered a collective international effort to safeguard important elements of our planet from destruction, similar to efforts with respect to the global environment. It can be considered to be a kind of applied global ethics.

The List attracts the attention of various actors:

- Experts on particularly important cultural and natural sites to be protected inform the general public. The placing of a Site on the List attracts considerable media attention. This is important because it propagates the information to a larger number of people. Indeed, inclusion in the List is considered to be a great honour for a nation, and accordingly receives a great deal of attention in press, radio, and TV. A higher number of visitors increases revenues from tourism.
- Public decision-makers are made aware of the great importance of particular cultural and natural sites within their country.
- The attention of potential donors is attracted. People who usually give money for cultural, artistic, and religious purposes may be willing to give more to Sites on the UNESCO List. New donors might also be attracted by the increased popularity.
- Firms may find ways and means to exploit the prominence of World Heritage Sites, either by catering for tourists visiting the sites or by sponsoring a particular World Heritage Site. In both cases, the administrators of the sites are likely to receive more money for their maintenance.

13.2.2 Protection

Involvement in the process of adding a Site to the World Heritage List strengthens a country's relationship with the international heritage movement. The World Heritage Commission offers technical help to preserve Sites on the List. Both tend also to be beneficial for sites that are not on the List or not yet on the List.

It should be noted that inclusion in the List is not accompanied by financial support from UNESCO.

13.3 Negative Aspects of the World Heritage List

Being on the UNESCO List may be subject to several undesirable consequences:

13.3.1 Questionable Selection

The selection of cultural and natural sites to be included in the List is strongly influenced by experts. They rely on their knowledge as art historians and conservators. In principle, every site included in the List is of equal value: the experts do not try to establish a ranking. No willingness-to-pay studies are undertaken to determine the value of a site, at least not in a manner considered satisfactory by cultural economists. Such studies seek to capture the utility gained by a representative sample in the population rather than the opinion of experts. It may well be argued that the general population often knows little or nothing about the sites in question and that therefore the stated willingness-to-pay of the population is of little relevance.

Being on the UNESCO List has been highly politicized, as many political and bureaucratic representatives of countries consider it a worthwhile goal from which they profit personally. As a consequence, selection is subject to political pressures and is not solely determined by criteria deemed to be "objective". Econometric research indeed suggests that more politically powerful countries have a better chance of putting their national sites on the List.

The questionable selection may be illustrated by some pertinent examples. In Switzerland, the old town of Berne is listed, but not the old towns of, for instance, Lucerne or Basel. The Benedictine Convent of St. John at Mustair and the monastery of St. Gallen are listed, but not the similarly important and ancient Benedictine monasteries of Engelberg and Einsiedeln. In all cases, it is difficult to argue why the latter are excluded. To provide an example from a totally different culture: The Djongs of Bhutan, which are of great art historic importance, are not listed, even though Bhutan has been a member of the Convention since 2001. Many more examples could be adduced.

13.3.2 Overextension

The number of sites on the UNESCO List has grown continuously over time and is now almost 1,200. This is a small number if one takes into account the richness of culture and nature on our planet.

It is difficult to see how this process can be slowed, let alone stopped. Provided the selection has been well made from the beginning, the newest additions are necessarily somewhat less well suited than the first ones (due to the law of decreasing marginal utility). However, ever more sites can be argued to fulfil the criteria. The problem is intensified because removals from the List are extremely rare. The case of countryside around Dresden is one of only two cases. The other is Oman's Arabian Oryx Sanctuary, which was removed from the List after the government of Oman reduced the sanctuary by 90% following the discovery of oil at the site.

Overextension takes a second form, an increasingly broad definition of what constitutes our planet's heritage. At the beginning, heritage was understood to be a specific historical monument, such as the Aachen Cathedral and the Chateau and Park of Versailles, or ensembles, such as Venice and its Lagoon or Stonehenge, Avebury, and associated sites. In addition, there is a List of World Heritage in Danger, comprising 31 properties. Later, Natural Sites were added, such as the Jungfrau-Aletsch region in the Swiss Alps and Lake Turkana National Parks in Kenya. Then Immaterial Cultural Heritage was added, such as the Carnival of Binche in Belgium and the Nooruz holiday in Kyrgyzstan.

13.3.3 Not Being on the List Means Being Less Valuable

A site not on the UNESCO List is, by definition, not quite first but rather second rate. Attention is directed to the Sites on the List. That a site not on the List is only second rate would be strongly denied by the World Heritage Commission and others involved in the selection process. But this is clearly understood to be the case for the general public, politicians, government bureaucracy, and potential donors. The tourist industry clearly understands that being on the List is a considerable advantage when advertising a tourist destination.

A second undesirable effect takes place when, due to the attention generated among politicians, bureaucrats, and firms, funds from other sites are reallocated to a Site on the List. An important prerequisite of the World Heritage Commission for being put on the List is that additional funds go into the preservation of the Sites. The loss of funds from non-UNESCO sites may well damage the heritage overall more than the increase in funds for the listed Sites, which find it much easier to attract money from private sponsors as well. This effect takes place as long as the total government budget and the funds from private firms for heritage projects are not raised to the same extent as additional money flowing to the listed Sites.

13.3.4 Attracting Destruction

Being on the World Heritage List makes an object interesting for three sets of actors.

In the case of not yet fully explored, excavated, and secured heritage sites, tomb robbers may gain a hint of how important the Site is. As a rule, the damage done is much worse than the robbery of objects because the Sites are destroyed and other objects mutilated.

More importantly listed Sites become a prominent target in war. As early as 1954, the Hague Convention for the Protection of Cultural Property in the Event of Armed Conflicts was drafted in response to the huge losses of cultural heritage suffered during World War II. The Blue Shield symbol was created to indicate cultural sites of special importance. While this may sometimes have preserved the object so designated, in many cases exactly the opposite has happened. Examples include the destruction of the ancient bridge at Mostar, the bombings of Sarajevo and Dubrovnik, and the obliteration of the great Buddhas at Bamiyan in Afghanistan. Terrorists, who strongly depend on media attention, seek highly visible and cherished iconic targets. The attribution of World Heritage status to a monument may well induce terrorists to attack and destroy it.

Another negative consequence of the increased popularity is the deterioration caused by the high numbers of visitors. This costly phenomenon has been observed at the most popular sites, such as Angkor Wat and Machu Picchu. The damage done by the huge masses of visitors is difficult to limit, is costly, and may reduce the authenticity of the site.

13.4 Alternatives to the UNESCO World Heritage List

The World Heritage List is often discussed as if there was no alternative to it. The UNESCO initiative tends to be presented as the only means by which the globe's cultural and natural heritage can be saved. In fact, there are various relevant alternatives.

13.4.1 No Intervention

The idea that cultural and natural sites would be destroyed or seriously hampered if they were not protected by the World Heritage List is untenable. Indeed, if the negative effects outlined above dominate the positive effects, it would even be preferable not to compile such a List. It can hardly be doubted that most of the well-known sites on the List would still exist if they were not on it. Aachen Cathedral and Versailles would not disappear. But it can be presumed that their state of preservation would possibly be worse if they were not on the List.

13.4.2 Use of the Market

"In the absence of external effects, the market could be trusted to preserve the globe's cultural and natural heritage." Few economists, not to speak of other people, would be prepared to argue that this is the case. Indeed, heritage is a case with strong positive external effects that markets do not, or insufficiently care for.

One possibility to use the market in order to efficiently preserve the public goods of world heritage is to introduce World Culture Certificates. The community of nations, as embodied by the United Nations, would have to agree on the Global Heritage List and to establish how many World Heritage Units each nation should save. Each World Heritage Site conserved would be acknowledged through the issuance of a tradable Certificate. The cost of a certificate would be lower the less expensive it would be to save a World Heritage Site. It is, therefore, advantageous to countries not only to concentrate on saving their national heritage, which may be very expensive due to decreasing returns, but also to seek sites where the World Heritage Certificates can be acquired most inexpensively. Countries and private firms are thus induced to seek sites where financial resources can be spent most productively. This leads to an efficient allocation of resources to preserve world heritage from a global point of view.

13.4.3 Competing Evaluations

The World Heritage Commission is not the only organization that provides lists of cultural and natural heritage. Probably one of the very first lists of major sites is the Seven Wonders of the Ancient World. The historian Herodotus made an early list of seven wonders, which served as a guidebook popular among the ancient Hellenic tourists. Nowadays, for-profit firms have long since established guides to the major heritage sites. Examples include tourist books attributing stars and similar ratings to the sites they find worth visiting and both scholarly and popular books devoted to informing people of the properties and landscapes they deem to be important, such as *1000 Places to See Before You Die*. To a significant extent, these lists overlap with the World Heritage List.

Many countries have extensive national lists of cultural and natural heritage sites. However, these lists often carry little weight when there are competing claims, and the respective objects are often poorly funded. But some developing countries have neither national lists nor the resources to protect, secure, and preserve their heritage. In these cases, the international effort of UNESCO is helpful. While the World Heritage Commission provides practically no funds to help in the preservation effort, it may be that inclusion in the List induces foreign nations, NGOs, and sponsoring firms to provide help.

13.4.4 Random Selection

One approach to reducing unwarranted political influence is to apply random selection. It is fair in the sense that every item has the same probability of being selected, which ensures a broad representation and reduces unwanted political intervention. In the form of demarchy (or lottocracy), this procedure was extensively used in classical Greek and Italian city-states such as Venice. Today, it is still used, for instance for jury services. For the selection of world heritage sites, two random mechanisms are possible.

The sites to be put on the World Heritage List can be chosen by lot from among all sites considered acceptable by the experts. Alternatively, all acceptable sites can be weighted by the classifications of the experts. Weight 3 could be given to those with recommended acceptance, weight 2 to those that have to be revised, and weight 1 to those with significant shortcomings. While this procedure would ensure representation of all acceptable sites, it makes it less attractive for governments to invest money and effort in advancing the claims of a property, because the final selection is beyond their influence.

A possible disadvantage may be that random selection does not provide the same prestige as selection by the UNESCO Heritage Committee. This problem could be circumvented by a second random mechanism. The selection is applied one step ahead, at the composition of the World Heritage Committee, which today takes the often-politicized decisions. The members of the committee could be selected by lot from the 193 member countries of the Convention. Random selection of the Committee members makes ex ante bargaining, strategic voting, and logrolling more difficult. Undesirable political influences can then be largely excluded, which should give more weight to an objective selection of sites based on the criteria agreed.

13.5 Alternative Approaches

The discussion shows that the effort by the UNESCO Heritage Commission to establish a List of World Heritage objects important to mankind has good and bad consequences. Strong positive effects are induced by the World Heritage List, in particular by drawing attention to prominent examples of our heritage and by providing protection and conservation to specific objects. There are also questionable aspects, such as the selection of sites not based on willingness-to-pay studies, and being subject to rent-seeking, in particular by the national interests pursued by politicians and bureaucrats but also by the commercial heritage industry. Among the negative consequences are the reduction of protection for sites not on the World Heritage List, the potential deterioration of the sites by excessive tourism, and the identification of an attractive goal for destruction in wars and by terrorists.

It is impossible to provide a general verdict, not least because an evaluation depends on preferences and the weights attributed to the various possible consequences. In a democratic system, these weights have to be determined in the political process.

What is possible, however, is to indicate the conditions under which the UNESCO List is particularly beneficial, and where and when it is important to actively involve the market and the national lists of heritage sites.

13.5.1 Beneficial World Heritage List

Inclusion into the World Heritage List is advantageous when one of the following six conditions obtain.

- *Undetected heritage sites.* The experts of UNESCO on culture and nature may be aware of particular heritage sites that are little known or unknown to the national decision-makers and market participants. This may be because the sites are difficult to access or are not yet excavated or developed. Suggesting to the respective governments to propose them for inclusion in the World Heritage List draws attention to the sites and helps to preserve them.
- *Commercially unexploited sites.* If access for tourists is very costly and burdensome and no facilities are available to host the visitors, or if the heritage sites are unfamiliar, inclusion in the World Heritage Commission List may attract funds from foreign governments and NGOs, and may start commercial development of the Site. The financial resources gained help to preserve the corresponding Sites.
- *Disregarding the need to preserve heritage important to mankind.* Nations and regions may not fully or sufficiently appreciate the value of cultural and natural sites as global public goods, but international experts and the World Heritage Commission do. This disregard may be due to insufficient knowledge, but presumably more often to ideologically biased views of what constitutes the planet's heritage. An example is the destruction of the Buddha statutes at Bamiyan in Afghanistan by the then-reigning Taliban. This act was undertaken for what the Taliban consider religious reasons. Furthermore, the importance of particular sites for the global public good of heritage may be overlooked or discounted.
  It is, of course, open whether inclusion in the World Heritage List is able to prevent the destruction of heritage sites by national governments and other actors. But it is known that authoritarian governments respond to international pressure as even they depend to some extent on good political and economic relationships with foreign countries.
- *Inadequate public resources.* The national and sub-national governments may want to preserve a particular heritage site but may lack the resources to do so because of extreme poverty. Another reason may be that the funds granted by the government for preserving heritage sites are wasted by incompetent or corrupt bureaucrats. Putting a site on the World Heritage List does not change these fundamental conditions, of course, but it may attract foreign funds less subject to waste.

- *Inadequate political control.* Civil wars and political unrest may make access and work on a heritage site dangerous or even impossible. Putting a site on the World Heritage List gains visibility and may at least partly overcome these problems.
- *Inadequate technical knowledge.* A country may be willing to preserve its cultural and natural heritage but may lack the technical expertise to undertake this task well. Once a Site is on the List, the exchange of technical knowledge is facilitated. Intensified contacts with the World Heritage Commission help to educate staff to preserve and manage the Sites.

13.5.2 Beneficial Alternatives

There are four important circumstances in which the use of market forces is preferable.

- *Popular sites.* Putting globally known and cherished properties such as the Coliseum, the Taj Mahal, and Stonehenge on the World Heritage List is unnecessary, as the market may be used to secure the funds necessary to preserve them. Using the price system with cultural and natural heritage requires adequate regulations to deal with external effects. However, the price system can be used in an intelligent way. Often, resistance by heritage experts against the market must be overcome, and sometimes those responsible for the heritage community are insufficiently educated or experienced to beneficially use pricing mechanisms. But today there are many examples that demonstrate that the price system may be helpful for conservation. A case in point is the many churches in Venice, which were mostly closed because there was no money to employ guards. Nowadays, the tourists must buy a ticket to visit these churches, which provides sufficient funds to reduce or fully prevent theft and destruction. Another example is Bhutan, which restricts the number of tourists allowed into the country by asking an entry fee and requires them to hire an official guide and driver, at considerable cost.
- *Weak externalities.* There are sites of cultural and natural heritage where externalities are weak and where therefore the price system can be expected to work quite well. The market can work directly via tourism or indirectly through sponsoring. When the externalities produced by the market are stronger, they must be combined with regulations reducing them. Examples include restrictions on the total number of visitors to a site, or on the noise and traffic pollution created.
- *Marked substitution effects induced by the inclusion in the World Heritage List.* Heritage sites whose positioning on the World Heritage List would lead to a neglect of other sites by the general public, the media, bureaucrats, and politicians and as a consequence to worse preservation efforts should not be proposed for the List. In such cases, national and regional lists are preferable as they are broader and include otherwise neglected sites.
- *Destruction potential.* In cases in which being on the World Heritage List can be expected to lead to a higher instance of destruction in armed conflicts and

by terrorists, it is reasonable to choose a lower profile. Decentralized protection through national and regional lists is better suited, since it attracts less attention.

The effort of UNESCO through the World Heritage Commission to establish a World Heritage List of the most treasured sites of humanity's culture and landscapes constitutes a great step towards preserving one of the most important global public goods on our planet. Precisely because it is an important enterprise, it must be critically analysed, and possible alternatives must be evaluated. My analysis suggests that the UNESCO Commissions approach is not the only viable option for safeguarding the valuable heritage humanity inherits from the past.

13.6 Conclusion

The UNESCO World Heritage List should not be taken as the only instrument for protecting important historic and natural sites. Other efforts to name and describe such sites should also be considered, in particular because the UNESCO List is subject to various biases. Governments know that a Site's presence on the List attracts large crowds of tourists and thus push to have as many Sites as possible on the List.

Efforts to protect the heritage of mankind should actively try to employ market forces. Most importantly, when sites are popular, they are preserved for commercial reasons. The better preserved a site is, the more opportunities are available for market activities, often also helping the local population to improve their incomes.

The UNESCO commission should take account of other ways to protect our common heritage. This is difficult, because the experts who compile the List want to keep their privileged positions. The whole process is to some extent constrained by bureaucratic and political considerations.

Related Literature

This chapter partly relies on

Frey BS (1997) The evaluation of cultural heritage. Some critical issues. In: Hutter H, Rizzo I (eds) Economic perspectives on cultural heritage. Palgrave Macmillan, London, pp 31–49

Frey BS, Pamini P (2010) World heritage: where are we? An empirical analysis. CESifo Working Paper No. 2919. Ifo Institute, Munich

Frey BS, Steiner L (2012) Pay as you go: a new proposal for museum pricing. Museum Manage Curatorship 27(2):223–235

The World Heritage List is presented in

UNESCO (2017) Operational guidelines for the implementation of the world heritage convention: https://whc.unesco.org/en/guidelines/

Important contributions from the economic point of view include

Benhamou F (1996) Is increased public spending for the preservation of historic monuments inevitable? The French case. J Cultural Econ 20(2):115– 131
Greffe X (1999) La gestion du patrimoine culturel. Anthropos, Paris

The relationship between heritage sites and terrorist attacks is analysed in

Frey BS, Rohner D (2007) Protecting cultural monuments against terrorism. Defence Peace Econ 18(3):245–252

An alternative list of valuable heritage sites is, for example, provided in

Schultze P (2003) 1000 places to see before you die: A traveller's life list. Workman Publishing, New York

Random procedures for selection are discussed in

Zeitoun H, Osterloh M, Frey BS (2014) Learning from ancient Athens: demarchy and corporate governance. Acad Manage Perspect 28(1):1–14

Chapter 14
Cultural Tourism

Abstract Mass tourism goes to major cultural heritage sites, to superstar museums, to festivals, and to blockbuster exhibitions of art. These visits have a major impact on the local economy, regions, and countries and are captured by impact studies. In contrast, the willingness-to-pay approach focuses on the net benefits created by visiting a cultural site. Many cultural sites tend to be overcrowded, leading to material damage to the structures, to a feeling of compression among visitors and the local population, and to a drastic loss of authenticity. Overcrowding of heritage sites can be counteracted in various ways to make visits agreeable and to reduce the damage inflicted.

Keywords Mass tourism · Superstar museums · Festivals · Blockbuster exhibitions · Most frequented cultural sites · Impact · Willingness-to-pay · European cultural capital · Happiness · Awards · Overcrowding · Entry price · Taxes · Exact copies

14.1 Types of Tourism

Cultural tourism has an old history. The classical Greeks and Romans visited Egypt to admire the pyramids; Venice has been an attraction much visited by tourists for centuries. In the 18th century, the Grand Tour was practically a requirement for young men of nobility. Before leaving home, they had to learn the languages of the countries they would visit. A local tutor was hired to monitor whether the young men made progress in their education.

Today, there is mass tourism to major cultural heritage sites, to superstar museums, to festivals, and to blockbuster exhibitions of art. Individual cultural tourists sometimes find it difficult to be able to visit, and especially to enjoy, such cultural locations and events. Before entering the Vatican's Saint Peter's Cathedral, one has to wait in a long queue and pass the security check.

Table 14.1 shows a selection of some cultural sites subject to mass tourism.

Table 14.1 is a specific selection; there are hundreds or thousands of other frequently visited cultural sites the world over.

B. S. Frey, *Economics of Art and Culture*, SpringerBriefs in Economics,
https://doi.org/10.1007/978-3-030-15748-7_14

Table 14.1 Some of the most frequently visited cultural sites

Ancient Rome, the Colosseum, the Vatican	Italy
Venice	Italy
Sagrada Família	Spain
Eiffel Tower	France
Empire State Building	United States of America
Pyramids of Giza	Egypt
Porto	Portugal

14.2 Economic Analysis

The tourists visiting cultural sites have a major impact on the local economy, regions, and countries. Cultural tourism strongly determines these areas' income, employment, and development.

14.2.1 Impact Versus Willingness-to-Pay Studies

The effects of cultural tourism on the economy can be captured by impact studies. These seek to measure the direct effect of the outlays by cultural tourists on goods and services, most importantly for transport, entry fees, accommodation, meals, and souvenirs. In addition, impact studies measure the additional effects of these initial expenditures on the economy. The more guests a hotel receives, the higher are its outlays for personnel and goods; thus, a multiplier effect is produced. As a result, the economic effects of a particular event, say a festival, are often taken to be large. They also raise tax revenues. The income gained from cultural tourists is at least partly used to preserve and to restore the cultural goods that in the first place attracted the visitors.

Impact studies, however, provide a problematic measure of the total benefits of cultural tourism. Visitors in general have mixed motives; they not only visit a city, region, or country solely because of the cultural attractions. People also want to enjoy the life of a city or the tranquillity of a country side, but it is also a "must" to visit the major cultural sites and performances. It is therefore incorrect to attribute all expenditures to the cultural sites at a location.

There may also be a displacement effect. Some tourists are likely to forgo a visit to another cultural site, so the overall effect is at best local but does not exist in the aggregate. Most importantly, impact studies only measure the additional revenue produced but disregard the inputs needed to create it. Nor are negative external effects considered. Mass cultural tourism in particular leads to increased pollution, noise, overcrowding, and other costs to local residents. These negative aspects have recently gained importance and have been reported in the media. Residents of cities such as

Venice, Amsterdam, Lucerne, and Barcelona have started to protest against excessive mass tourism.

In contrast to impact studies, the willingness-to-pay approach focuses on the net utility created by a cultural site. It seeks to capture its value above and beyond the effects reflected by markets. The visitors are asked to state how much they would be willing to spend to visit a particular cultural site such as Saint Peter's Cathedral in the Vatican. Their answer takes into account both the benefits and the costs of a visit. Such studies typically ask both the visitors and the local residents. Consequently, the negative external effects are taken into account.

Another approach is to ask the level of life satisfaction due to cultural tourism. This has so far only been undertaken for local residents and a specific cultural event, namely the nomination of a European Cultural Capital. It emerges that the life satisfaction, or happiness, of the people living in a city rises when that city is nominated but falls in the year the city is a Cultural Capital. The negative effects in higher prices and reduced amenities seem to outweigh the benefits experienced.

14.2.2 Attracting Cultural Tourists

Many communities and countries make considerable efforts to attract cultural tourists, not least because they have higher average incomes and are prepared to spend more money than other types of visitors. It also adds to the prestige of a location if it features important cultural sites.

The Basque town Bilbao was characterized by declining industry. When the Guggenheim Museum, designed by Frank Gehry, opened in 1997, Bilbao became a most attractive tourist destination, and the city was transformed. Now, tourists also admire its old town, an aspect almost totally neglected before. Many cities all over the world attempt to replicate this beneficial cultural and economic effect. A remarkable example in Spain is Malaga, which tourists used to pass by quickly on their way to the Costa del Sol. Now, the town features various significant art museums, among which one devoted to Pablo Picasso, who was born there. Such newly installed museums help the Spanish economy to diversify, which matters as the concentration on beach tourism appears to be levelling off. As yet, only a small minority of foreign tourists come mostly for culture, but the absolute number is rising quickly.

The world's leading collection of contemporary Chinese art is to be on display at the M+ Museum for Visual Arts and Culture in Hong Kong. The new museum, due to open in 2019, was designed by Herzog & de Meuron and owes its collection to the Swiss collector and philanthropist Uli Sigg. The Cultural District of Abu Dhabi intends to house a number of world-class cultural assets. Frank Gehry designed the Louvre Abu Dhabi Museum of Art and Civilization and the Guggenheim Abu Dhabi contemporary arts museum. In addition, there are plans for the Zayed National Museum to be designed by Norman Foster, a maritime museum designed by Tadao Ando, and a performing arts centre by Zaha Hadid. These new cultural locations are likely to become major magnets for cultural tourists.

Bequeathing awards also attracts cultural tourists. The corresponding ceremonies are attended by politicians and people important in culture and are reported in the media. They inform people about particularly attractive destinations. In Switzerland, for instance, each year a commune or city considered to best preserve their heritage receives the Wakker Prize. In Italy, the organization Borghi medievali più belli d'Italia names small communes less well known than famous historic cities such as Florence, Pisa, or Siena. Such enterprises help to diversify cultural mass tourism. However, if they are successful, they can lead to overcrowding of such small places. This is already the case in, for instance, San Gimignano in Italy and Rothenburg ob der Tauber in Germany.

Another recent enterprise to attract cultural tourists is to rent out an ancient house or castle for a restricted period of time. In a few cases, museums allow tourists to stay overnight in their premises. An example is the Fondazione Casa-Museo D'Oro Lambertenghi located in Tirano in the Italian province of Sondrio.

14.2.3 Dealing with Overcrowding

Many cultural sites are subject to mass tourism and tend to be overcrowded, leading to material damage to the structures, to a feeling of congestion of visitors and the local population, and to a drastic loss of authenticity. As early as 1817, Stendhal remarked that "Florence is a museum full of foreigners". There are sites that tourists must visit at all cost. Tourist guides and rankings similar to the Michelin stars in gastronomy indicate, or even dictate, what tourists "must" see. The fact that other tourists overrun such locations is taken as an indication that one has chosen well. Collecting sites at the top of rankings has become the main purpose of travelling for many. Taking pictures, and in particular selfies, has become many tourists' main goal. This even holds if the sites are reproductions. Neuschwanstein in Bavaria, built in 1869 by King Ludwig II, is an idealized medieval castle built in the Romanesque revival. Since it was opened to the public in 1886, more than 60 million people have visited it. In summer, it receives up to 6000 visitors per day.

In the near future, the number of cultural tourists is likely to increase, probably greatly. As a result of rising incomes, visitors from China and India can increasingly afford to see the cultural highlights in Europe. This tendency is increased by longer life expectancy, better education, and globalization. Many tourist cities of culture, such as Florence and Siena, already have more visitors than local residents. To visit the churches, palaces, museums, and even squares has become cumbersome, reducing the benefits of cultural tourism.

Overcrowding of heritage sites can be counteracted in various ways to make visits agreeable and to reduce the damage inflicted:

- The visiting crowds can be directed to less well-known locations offering similar cultural attractions. Many towns and regions stage musical festivals well worth seeing but little known. By informing tourist organizations and the media, the flow of cultural tourists can be diversified.

- Cultural locations can raise taxes and the price of public transport or parking spaces to reduce the inflow of visitors. Churches rightly want to distinguish themselves from museums and therefore refrain from asking an entry price. In fact, to a very large extent they serve as museums. There are few tourists who visit San Marco Cathedral in Venice to pray, but many admire the wonderful structure, mosaics, and paintings. The problem can be solved to some extent by offering tourists a ticket enabling them to visit various churches. In that case, no monetary payment is required to enter a church. This is the solution taken by the Church in Venice.
- Another approach to reducing mass cultural tourism is to ask a price to enter a location. This procedure should be easy to undertake in the case of Venice, where most visitors enter through the Piazzale Roma. The huge cruisers, some disgorging up to 6000 people into the city at the same time, could be asked a higher price than individual tourists. Even if most cultural cities can be entered in many different ways, progress in digitization should allow also an entry price to be demanded.
- An extreme way to safeguard cultural sites from an excessive number of visitors is to exactly copy the most important parts and to locate these copies at another place more suitable for mass tourism. Around 60,000–70,000 tourists visit Venice per day. This is more than the number of inhabitants in the city. Not surprisingly, the major attractions, such as the Duomo di San Marco, and its square, and the Palazzo dei Dogi are extremely overcrowded. The excess numbers of visitors damages the city in a number of ways. In order to reduce this damage, the major churches, palaces, squares, monuments, and canals of Venice could be exactly duplicated at a location somewhere else on the coast. Modern technology could be employed to make the visit to the replica more attractive. The buildings could, for instance, be populated by holograms of important people of Venice's glorious past, such as illustrious doges. The famous carnival could be made vivid by populating the squares with actors dressed in costumes of the past. Crucial historical events could be re-enacted. It can be expected that many tourists would prefer to visit the replica. If such a plan were implemented the original city of Venice would be less damaged than is the case today.

At first sight, this idea seems lunatic. However, there are examples of this procedure proving successful. The extraordinary prehistoric paintings in the caves of Lascaux in France and Altamira in Spain were closed because the breath of the immense numbers of visitors led to severe damage. New caves were drilled nearby, and the paintings exactly copied. The visitors are aware that the caves are copies but do not mind entering them, not least because the paintings are more clearly visible. The idea of producing replicas of cultural icons has also been undertaken in Las Vegas and to an even larger extent in Macao, where part of Venice and the Canale Grande have been rebuilt. The Eiffel Tower has been copied dozens of times in China, though at smaller scales than the real one. In these cases, no exact replicas are provided, though this is possible using modern technology.

14.3 Conclusion

Cultural tourism has become a mass phenomenon and is likely to increase further in the future. Yet overcrowding of heritage sites can be counteracted in various ways to make visits agreeable and to reduce the damage inflicted. Visitors can be redirected to less well-known locations, taxes can be increased, and entry fees imposed.

A somewhat unorthodox approach would be to rebuild the most visited and damaged sites in a more suitable location. With today's technology, the most important historic parts can be copied exactly, so that after some time tourists and other people no longer see any difference from the original. In addition, holograms and other digital features can be used to raise the copies' attractiveness. This procedure has been successfully undertaken to save sites subject to damage by large numbers of cultural visitors.

Related Literature

Early contributions include

Gapinski JH (1988) Tourism's contribution to the demand for London's lively arts. Appl Econ 20(7):957–968

Mossetto G (1992) L'economia delle città d'arte: Modelli di sviluppo a confronte, politiche e strumenti di intervento, Etaslibri, Milan

More recent contributions are, for example

D'Eramo M (2017) Il selfie del mondo. Indagine sull'età del turismo, Feltrinelli, Milano

Hughes HL (2000) Arts, entertainment and tourism. Butterworth-Heineman, Oxford

Scott AJ (2000) The cultural economy of cities: essays on the geography of image-producing industries. Sage, London

An analysis using happiness data to capture the net benefits produced by cultural sites is

Steiner L, Frey BS, Hotz S (2015) European capitals of culture and life satisfaction. Urban Stud 52(2):374–394

Part IV
Cultural Policy

Chapter 15
Public Support of the Arts

Abstract The supply of art deviates in several respects from the ideal of a well-functioning market. Deficits continually increase. On the demand side, problems are caused by merit goods, external benefits in production and consumption, and public goods. People value the options, existence, bequest, education, and prestige connected to the arts. These failures seem to speak in favour of government stepping in. However, government intervention is also liable to failure. Decisions taken in the political process may deviate systematically from the preferences of the population. Nonetheless, citizens are quite willing to support the arts with substantial funds if asked to in popular initiatives and referenda.

Keywords Well-functioning market · Market failure · Declining cost · Productivity lag · Income distribution · Merit goods · External benefits · External cost · Public goods · Non-use values · Existence value · Bequest value · Education value · Prestige value · Government intervention · Government support · Art expenditures · Tax expenditures · Donations · Preferences · Constitution · Democracy · Popular initiatives · Popular referenda

15.1 Government Support of the Arts

Governments have been closely involved in the arts throughout history. The church, kings and queens, other aristocrats, and city councils were the main supporters of the arts up to the 20th century. Some private patrons and educational establishments financed libraries, archives, and museums. Nevertheless, some artists used the private market to earn income. Painters sold their works to private collectors. In the 18th and early 19th centuries, composers such as Wolfgang Amadeus Mozart and Ludwig van Beethoven charged an admission price for their public concerts. In the last century, democratic governments increasingly engaged in patronage roles. They created institutions such as arts councils and ministries of culture, mainly supporting painting and sculpture, theatres and opera houses, and classical music.

B. S. Frey, *Economics of Art and Culture*, SpringerBriefs in Economics,
https://doi.org/10.1007/978-3-030-15748-7_15

15.1.1 Direct Government Expenditures

The extent of direct subsidies to the arts and culture between countries is difficult to measure. What counts as "art expenditure" or "expenditures for culture" and what falls in the domain of "government" differs considerably between countries. It very much depends on the definitions used. Therefore, no reliable comparisons are available. However, it is known that countries spend widely differing amounts of money on direct public expenditures for the arts. The United States spend much less, and Finland and Germany substantially more, than other countries. The source of public support also differs widely. Thus, for example, in Ireland nearly 90% comes from the central government, while in Germany it is less than 10%, the bulk coming from the Länder and cities.

15.1.2 Indirect Public Support of the Arts

A substantial proportion of the aid given to the art is organized in an indirect way: people donating money to the arts can deduct it from their tax bill. Firms supporting cultural activities and items do not have to pay any revenue or profit tax on such expenditures. The higher the applicable marginal tax rate, the less costly it is to give to the arts. The extent of tax deductibility for the arts varies greatly between countries and depends on many different conditions. In many countries, such as the United States, this form of aid is substantial and is often larger than direct expenditures.

15.2 Arguments for the Public Support of the Arts

An economic analysis of support for the arts and culture focuses on the question of whether the private market misallocates resources in this domain, and in particular why too little art is provided if left to the market system.

It is useful to distinguish between the supply and demand sides.

15.2.1 Market Failure on the Supply Side

The supply of art may deviate in four major respects from the ideals of a well-functioning market:

- *Imperfect competition*. Quasi-monopolistic actors characterize the market for many cultural goods and services. They offer smaller quantities at higher prices above marginal costs than competitive suppliers would. The government might correct this market failure by supporting additional supply. However, not all art

supply is subject to imperfect competition. Auctions of art objects are an example of an almost perfectly competitive market.
- *Declining cost.* The production of art may be subject to increasing returns to scale. Additional quantities may be produced at lower average cost, in which case marginal cost is lower than average cost. However, the condition of efficient pricing, namely that price equals marginal cost, produces a loss. If the government wants to impose marginal cost pricing, it must support suppliers by covering the difference between marginal and average cost.
- *Productivity lag.* Suppliers in the live performing arts may be subject to the cost disease. They find it difficult, if not impossible, to increase labour productivity but have to increase pay in accordance with the rest of the economy. As a result, deficits continually increase. If these conditions hold in the long run, the performing arts can only exist if the government subsidizes the difference between lagging labour productivity and general wage increases.
- *Income distribution.* Artists are, on average, less well off than other members of society. Egalitarian arguments may constitute a reason for government to support individuals active in the cultural sector.

15.2.2 Market Failures on the Demand Side

Too little art is supplied if markets do not reflect all the preferences of individuals for enjoying art. The following types of demand are not fully, or only partially, reflected by markets:

- *Merit goods.* From the point of view of society as a whole, it may be considered desirable to provide larger quantities of cultural goods and services than the individual consumers would wish to purchase on the market. If that is so, consumer preferences are not accepted. The political decision-makers have to decide according to "inherent" worth or to what the majority of the population wants. The idea of merit goods clashes with the basic proposition in economics that the consumers know best what suits them. In many cases, merit wants are brought forward by suppliers of cultural services not for intrinsic reasons but to gain public support.
- *External benefits in production and consumption.* The provision of artistic activities may yield benefits to individuals and firms not integrated in the production process. They reap benefits for which they do not pay, and which art producers in a market therefore disregard. Similarly, part of the benefits of artistic production may go to individuals and firms that do not pay for such consumption, and which therefore do not influence the production decisions in art markets. In both cases, production is too small compared to what is socially optimal.
- *Non-market demand.* People may value the option of visiting an artistic production though, in fact, they never spend any money on actually attending one. People may also value the existence of an activity. Some people may not themselves value art, but consider it a bequest for future generations. In many cases, artistic production

is closely identified with national identity, prestige, and social cohesion. Artistic production may also contribute to a broad liberal education among the participants. The experimental nature of some artistic endeavours may foster innovation and risk taking in parts of society. The producers of art are not fully compensated in monetary terms for these benefits created. As a result, they are sometimes not able to provide the cultural activity at all, or only on a smaller scale than would be socially optimal.

- *Art as a public good.* Art may be of a collective nature; nobody can be excluded from enjoying it, including those not paying. Moreover, the consumption of one person does not reduce the consumption of others. The suppliers are incompletely compensated for their efforts, so supply is lower than socially optimal.
  In contrast, the cultural consumption provided by, say, theatres, opera houses, or museums, is not a public good, because people not paying may be excluded. There is also rivalry in consumption. Customers taking a seat occupy a space that is no longer available to others.
- *Insufficient information.* Consumers are often poorly informed about the supply of art. This argument has often been used to support government intervention. The question is on what basis politicians, public officials, and experts can claim that they know better what a specific item of art is worth. Often, such people merely defend their own interest; due to their backgrounds, they are able to construct seemingly convincing arguments for public support. For instance, the directors of theatres are rarely, if ever, observed arguing that some of their funds should instead be devoted to, say, a museum.
- *Irrationality.* Individuals may be subject to behavioural anomalies when they act in the area of culture, because the arts elude easy and clear definitions and categorizations. Individuals may underrate the utility provided by culture. The government should therefore support the arts to compensate the lack in demand.
- *Income distribution.* It can well be argued that the consumption of cultural goods should be open to all members of society and should not be reserved for the rich. Consequently, the government should support the arts in order to make its consumption available to those who are not able to spend much money consuming them.

15.2.3 Comparative View

Even if market failures have been theoretically and empirically identified for the arts, they constitute at best a *prima facie* argument for public support. It must be taken into account that government intervention is also liable to failure. The economics of politics (Public Choice) discusses many reasons why decisions taken in the political process may deviate systematically from the preferences of the population. Most importantly, politicians are motivated by the need to be re-elected rather than by any direct incentive to provide welfare-maximizing cultural policies. As elections take place only every fourth or fifth year, voters can only insufficiently control them.

Politicians tend to develop into a class of their own, and to a considerable extent decide according to their own tastes to what extent, and how, culture is to be supported. Political failures are also introduced by the behaviour of public officials, who due to their informational advantages have large discretionary power to implement a cultural policy of their liking. In general, they prefer to promote well-established cultural institutions providing classical art, such as opera houses performing pieces by Verdi, Mozart, Puccini, and Rossini. In contrast, more controversial and experimental art finds it more difficult to gain public support. Politicians, who depend on public opinion and re-election, are afraid of scandals, which are more likely to be provoked by outsiders in art.

Indirect aid via tax expenditures is less subject to such pressures and may result in more diversified support of artistic activities. At the same time, both politicians and public officials are exposed to the influence of pressure groups. As a result, they tend to favour well-organized cultural suppliers. In most cases this results in concentrating funds on a few large and well-established cultural suppliers, such as opera houses, national theatres, and orchestras. In contrast, new, unorthodox, and experimental art suppliers find it difficult to attract much public aid, which tends to hamper creativity in the arts.

To get a balanced view, it is necessary to compare the extent of market and political failures in cultural issues.

15.3 Constitutional Issues For and Against the Public Support of the Arts

The notion of market failure seems to favour government support for the arts. But the world is always imperfect. Compared to an ideal situation, the idea of failure is of little relevance, because the whole economy and society is dominated by failures. It does not make much sense to identify the extent to which the cultural sector deviates from ideal market conditions or ideal political ones, as all sectors in society do so to some extent.

A more useful approach is to directly compare the sectors with each other. The question then becomes whether the cultural sector receives more or less public support than other sectors, and whether such support improves the welfare of the population.

The first part of the question is easy to answer: the cultural sector does receive considerable support from the government, but it is small compared to other sectors, such as agriculture, education, transport, and defence.

The second part of the question cannot be answered directly, at least as long as it is agreed that there is no such thing as a collective social welfare function, which would enable us to evaluate and compare the performance of the various sectors. As such an evaluation is not possible in an empirically meaningful way, it is useful to move to a constitutional level of analysis. Public aid to a sector must be subject to a generally accepted decision process. In a democracy, the citizens must approve such support. In a representative democratic system, the decisions taken by a duly elected parliament and government are taken as legitimate, even if they are not perfect. In a democracy in which the population exercises direct participation rights via popular referenda, such as various states of the USA, in Australia, and in Switzerland, the voters' response to specific propositions, and the corresponding level of support for the arts, is taken as decisive. Empirical research indicates that the citizens are quite willing to support the arts with substantial funds if asked to in referenda. The fear often raised that the population will reject supporting the arts by public means does not materialize at all. Whatever has been decided with respect to the support of the arts and other sectors in the democratic political process must be assumed to fulfil the wishes of the population.

In contrast, when the democratic process is violated, or when the decision process is taken in an authoritarian or dictatorial way, public support for the arts (or for any other sector of the economy) does not reflect the wishes of the population. In that case, the art that is produced conforms to what the people in political power consider to be art. Only in the case of highly cultured rulers (an example is the Medici family in Renaissance Italy) will the art publicly supported be of lasting value. In the other cases, the activities that are promoted are those of artists who produce to the liking of the authoritarian rulers. An example is the socialist realism commanded by Stalin.

An important constitutional characteristic concerning the public support of art is whether decision-making is centralized or takes place in a federal system of government. In the latter case, art suppliers do not depend solely on one public authority but can approach several public donors. This raises the opportunities and incentives for innovative art.

15.4 Conclusion

Cultural producers have to deal with the cost disease, but they have various options to overcome the problem. They can increase labour productivity by more capital-intensive production and rely more strongly on digitization.

Faced by high costs relative to revenue, cultural suppliers have several strategies to avoid running a loss. Important ones include raising revenue by ancillary activities, such as running a shop, cafeteria, and a restaurant, renting out the premises for other activities, and seeking support from private and corporate sponsors. Many art organizations have demonstrated that a great deal of income can be generated in these ways. The opportunities to do so are, however, limited. Many art institutions have little scope to engage in such profit making. This is the case for many local and regional suppliers of culture, who nevertheless produce worthwhile art. Commercialization may threaten the quality of art. Cultural producers should not lose sight of what they stand for and try to become social entertainers. The profit-making potential of this strategy is also limited as the cultural suppliers may lose their non-profit status. This holds most obviously for museum shops run outside the museums' premises, say in large shopping centres. If their non-profit status is lost, they become subject to additional taxes, and donations are no longer be deducted from taxable income. Both consequences would threaten the very existence of many, if not most, cultural suppliers and would therefore have counterproductive effects.

Relying solely on the market to provide goods and services in the cultural sector certainly does not lead to a beneficial situation. The art market in several respects does not function in a satisfactory way.

Turning to government to solve all the problems is, however, naïve. While it has many instruments available for directly and indirectly supporting the arts, decisions taken in the representative political process tend to systematically deviate from the preferences of the population. Politicians are motivated by the need for re-election rather than to provide welfare-maximizing cultural policies for society. Public officials are also motivated strongly by their own interests.

One option for at least partially overcoming these shortcomings of the decision process in representative democracies is to allow citizens to participate directly in the political process by popular initiatives and referenda. Empirical research indicates that the citizens are quite willing to support the arts with substantial funds if asked to decide in referenda.

Related Literature

This chapter partly follows

Frey BS (2003) Public support. In: Towse R (ed) A handbook of cultural economics. Edward Elgar, Cheltenham UK and Northampton, MA, pp 389–398

The market failure approach is developed in many textbooks and readers on cultural economics.

Specific monographs dealing with the public support of the arts include, for example,

Schuster JM (1998) Neither public nor private: the hybridization of museums. J Cult Econ 22(2–3):127–150

Towse R (ed) (1997) Cultural economics: the arts, the heritage and the media industries. Edward Elgar, Cheltenham UK and Lyme, US

West EG (1985) Subsidizing the performing arts. Ontario Economic Council, Toronto

Arguments against direct public support for the arts are advanced by

Cowen T (1998) In praise of commercial culture. Harvard University Press, Cambridge, MA
Grampp WD (1989) Pricing the priceless. Art, artists and economics. Basic Books, New York

That citizens are prepared to support the arts, even if they do not personally engage in them, is shown in

Frey BS, Pommerehne WW (1995) Public expenditure on the arts and direct democracy: the use of referenda in Switzerland. Cult Policy 2(1):55–65
Schulze GG, Ursprung HW (2000) La donna e mobile—or is She? Voter preferences and public support for the performing arts. Public Choice 102(1–2):129–147

Chapter 16
Does Art Make Us Happy?

Abstract Empirical evidence reveals that artists are happier than similar other people, and that participation in cultural activities raises life satisfaction. It may be that the causation runs in the opposite direction, namely that happy people become artists, and that they attend more cultural occasions. However, there are strong indications that this reverse effect is not dominant and that art indeed makes artists and consumers happy.

Keywords Artists · Participation in cultural activities · Life satisfaction · Unhappy artist · Measuring happiness · Attendance · Leisure

16.1 Happiness in the Arts

Quite obviously, art makes some people happy. It provides deeply satisfying new insights and experiences. Mass visits to museums and special exhibitions provide strong support for this observation. Art collectors are fond of emphasizing how much pleasure they derive from art.

On the other hand, art is also connected to unhappiness. We know of artists that have been deeply depressed all their lives, and some even committed suicide. The tragedy of painters such as Vincent van Gogh, or authors such as Heinrich von Kleist and Ernest Hemingway, lends itself well to the formation of legends and the production of Hollywood films. Some artists have consciously chosen to adapt this habitus, knowing that the "unhappy artist" is well received by the public.

16.2 Measuring Happiness

Modern economics and psychology have made great advances in survey methods. It is now possible to measure the extent of subjective life satisfaction, or in short, happiness. A random selection of people is asked the question: "Taken overall, how satisfied are you with the life you lead?" on a scale ranging from 0, indicating that

B. S. Frey, *Economics of Art and Culture*, SpringerBriefs in Economics,
https://doi.org/10.1007/978-3-030-15748-7_16

one is “deeply unhappy”, to 10, indicating that one is “totally happy”. Most people are quite satisfied with their lives; they state a value between 6 and 8.

The survey results correspond well with objective observations. People who state that they are happy laugh more, have fewer problems at their workplace and in their families, are more communicative and optimistic, and are less prone to committing suicide.

16.3 Happy Artists

The empirical evidence provided in Chap. 4 on the Artist’ Labour Market shows that, on average, artists are more satisfied with their lives than are people of similar education, income, and age. This, of course, does not exclude the possibility that some artists are unhappy, but it is also true that some artists are very happy.

16.4 Participation in Cultural Activities

Whether a person consumes artistic activities is captured by this question: “How often do you visit cultural activities such as concerts or theatre plays in your leisure time?” The answers range from “never”, through “less than once a month”, and “once a month” to “weekly”. One study in Germany revealed that more than half of the respondents did not attend any cultural activity at all. Almost 90% of the German population is not actively engaged as consumers of art, let alone as producers. A tiny share of the population in Germany—which is proud of being a country of culture—attends cultural activities every week. These findings indicate that art does not directly involve the large majority of people, and that strong efforts must be undertaken to change this situation.

16.5 The Relationship Between Art and Happiness

Statistics allow us to capture whether consumers of cultural activities are happier than those who abstain.

Figure 16.1 shows the relationship between culture, happiness, and life satisfaction in Germany, both overall and in leisure time.

The figure reveals a clear positive relationship. People attending cultural activities more often are much more satisfied with their lives than those who rarely or never consume art. Those who “never” attend any cultural event indicate a self-declared life satisfaction of 6.7, and are far from the maximum of 10. In contrast, those consuming an art activity “weekly” indicate a happiness level of 7.3; they are much more satisfied

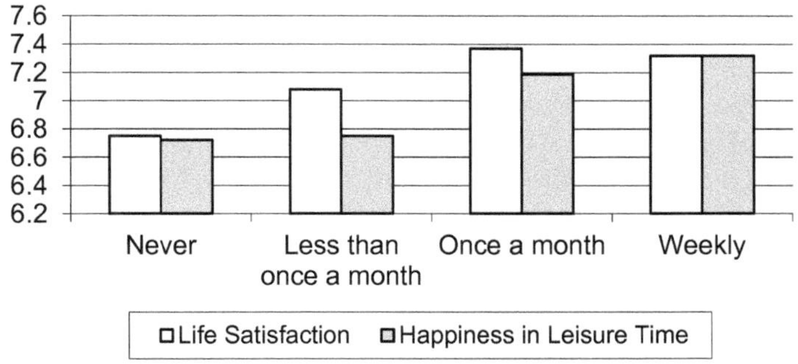

Fig. 16.1 Attendance at cultural activities, happiness in leisure time, and subjective life satisfaction, Germany 1985–1999. *Source* Frey (2008a)

with the lives they lead. The positive relationship between happiness and engaging in the arts is well established.

Figure 16.1 also shows that people who visit cultural events more often are happier in their leisure time.

It can be argued that the positive relationship between art and happiness is not direct but is produced by quite different determinants. People with higher incomes both are happier and attend more cultural events. This relationship is well documented by empirical research.

To separate the possible effects, the relationship between participation in the arts and happiness has been analysed in econometric studies that take into account determinants of happiness in addition to income. The result revealed in the raw data of Fig. 16.1 is confirmed: The positive relationship between attending cultural activities and happiness remains intact.

16.6 Reverse Causality?

The positive connection between attending art events and happiness leaves open whether art makes happy, or whether happy people visit more art activities. Statistical research does not allow us to provide a definite answer; most likely both directions of causation exist at the same time. As happier people are more open, more inquisitive, and more socially minded, they are more inclined to visit cultural events than people who are less satisfied with their lives. At the same time, art can certainly contribute to happiness as it opens new insights and experiences. The latter effect does not apply to all kinds of art. People attending a deeply pessimistic theatrical play or viewing negative or destructive paintings and sculptures are probably less happy than before. But to attend a wonderful opera or theatrical play, to visit an attractive art collection, to admire beautiful cathedrals, palaces and beautifully kept gardens certainly lifts spirits and contributes to happiness.

16.7 Conclusion

Happiness is determined by many factors, such as income, social relationships, physical and psychological health, and favourable political conditions. Empirical evidence suggests that art also contributes significantly to subjective well-being.

Related Literature

Frey BS (2008a) Cities, culture and happiness. *ETHOS, World Cities Summit Issue,* June 2008:102–111

A modest, but significant effect of attending art events on happiness has been found for the United Kingdom by

Hand C (2018) Do the arts make you happy? A quantile regression approach. J Cult Econ 42(2):271–286

A general survey of research on subjective life satisfaction is provided in

Frey BS (2018) Economics of happiness. Springer Briefs in Economics, Springer, Cham

A more extensive discussion is provided in

Frey BS (2008b) Happiness—a revolution in economics. MIT Press, Cambridge, MA
Frey BS, Stutzer A (2002) Happiness and economics. How the economy and institutions affect human well-being. Princeton University Press, Princeton

www.ingramcontent.com/pod-product-compliance
Ingram Content Group UK Ltd.
Pitfield, Milton Keynes, MK11 3LW, UK
UKHW020147290926
15471UKWH00004B/735

9783030157470